CLINICAL SUPERVISION

Skills for Substance Abuse Counselors

CLINICAL SUPERVISION

Skills for Substance Abuse Counselors

David J. Powell, PH.D

Eastern Area Alcohol Education and Training Program, Inc.
Bloomfield, Connecticut

HUMAN SCIENCES PRESS

72 Fifth Avenue, NEW YORK, NY 10011 • 3 Henrietta Street, LONDON, WC2E 8LU

72 Fifth Avenue, New York, New York 10011

Printed in the United States of America
0 1 2 3 4 5 6 7 8 9

Library of Congress Cataloging in Publication Data

Powell, David J.
Clinical supervision.

Includes index.
1. Drug abuse counseling—Study and teaching.
2. Alcoholism counseling—Study and teaching.
I. Title
RC564.P68 616.8'6'06 LC 79-20586
ISBN 0-87705-406-1

To Barbara

Contents

List of Figures and Tables

FIGURES

Tables

Acknowledgments

Many have helped me in the preparation of this book. This project was initiated as a result of workshops conducted for schools of alcohol studies and counselor training programs, especially the clinical supervisor workshop of Virginia Commonwealth University. I am grateful to Dr. Marcia Lawton for inspiring me to begin writing.

My sincere thanks to Robert Fuller, the closest friend a person could have, who also happens to be an excellent clinical supervisor. He collaborated on the development and delivery of the training programs which sparked the origin of the book. For the hours spent in preparation, and the fun in presenting the material at various workshops, a note of special appreciation to Bob.

A special debt of gratitude is due to Dr. Robert Stuckey, whose words of wisdom I hope I will always remember: "No matter how far you progress in this field, no matter how much money you earn, or how important your title, always remember you are in this field because of the life changes that occur in others and yourself."

But above all, I want to express my thanks to my wife, Barbara Boss Powell, for her hours of proofing dangling participles and run-on sentences, and her continued help, support, and encouragement in having this work published. For her lost weekends and evenings, a very special thanks.

Foreword

Alcoholism counseling in the United States has a long and interesting history. People who were able to overcome their own alcoholism have often felt the urge to share that recovery with their still-suffering counterparts. This process of sharing goes back in American history at least as far as 1840, when a group of six friends in Baltimore, Maryland founded the Washington Temperance Society. This group, generally known as the Washingtonians, included many recovered alcoholics. Although they promoted abstinence by all, the Washingtonians also worked successfully towards the "reformation of drunkards" through kindness, concern, and respect, techniques widely accepted as basic for all counseling. The Washingtonian Hospital in Boston, founded by members of the Society in 1857, still functions as an addictions treatment center.

The years since the decline of the Washington Temperance Society at the turn of the century saw many recovered alcoholics assume the role of "lay therapist" in a variety of situations. These included religious groups and missions, small "rest homes" or rehabilitation centers, in the offices of independent practitioners, counselors working with physicians or in medical facilities, early industrial programs, court and prison programs, and others. As many of these gifted, independently working counselors refined their skills, they also developed a number of "systems" and "methods" for counseling alcoholics, which constituted, at one time, all the literature on addiction counseling. The 1939 book by Strecker and Chambers is an example.

The founding of Alcoholics Anonymous in the 1930s and its explosive growth since that time has led to the availability of an increasing number of recovered alcoholics with experience in "twelve-stepping" (that is, applying in their lives that part of the twelve steps of the AA program which involves "carrying the message of recovery" to other alcoholics). It was inevitable that some of these people would choose careers in counseling and would be called upon to staff the alcoholism treatment facilities developed since the 1950s. But counseling and "twelve-stepping" are not synonymous, and both formal training and formal supervision in counseling skills were needed. The development and growth of drug abuse treatment programs in the 1960s and 1970s created a parallel need for trained addiction counselors. Many who assumed this role were themselves former drug abusers.

The alcoholism and drug abuse field were quicker to perceive and respond to the need for counselor training than for organized supervision. It is the latter need to which this volume addresses itself. The questions posed in Chapter 2 may seem absurd at first, until the reader realizes that adequate clinical supervision for addiction counselors today is the exception rather than the rule in the field.

In guiding us step-by-step through the theory and practice of counselor supervision as it applies to the field of addictive diseases, the author not only informs and instructs us, but offers us the arguments we need to convince others of the value of clinical supervision. He offers models of adequate supervisory programs that can be instituted in our agencies. He offers supervisory and evaluative tools and criteria for their use.

This book should be of value to those of us struggling to provide the kind of supervision that assures quality of care to our patients. It should be of even greater value to those of us who have not yet begun to address this issue in an organized and effective way.

SHEILA B. BLUME, M.D.

President,
American Medical Society on Alcoholism

Director,
New York State Division on Alcoholism
Albany, New York

Introduction

Once upon a time there was a young aspiring wiseman called Ernie. He was most gifted at providing council, advice, and wise sayings to those in distress. He received his training under the tutelage of his distant relative, Morris the Magician. From throughout the kingdom, people would come to Ernie for help for a diverse range of problems, such as what to wear to a beheading, how to sober up for a joust after a night of bacchanalian debauchery, and what to do when one discovers that one's wife has made a number of duplicate sets of keys to her chastity belt. Ernie became known throughout the land as an excellent counselor, and nobleman.

One day, the King asked Ernie to become the Head Wiseman, the ruler of the largest serfdom in the kingdom. As a ruler he would have to administer and manage the serfdom, and supervise the other wisemen. "I have no experience as a ruler," said Ernie to the King. "I am a simple wiseman. I do not know how to supervise the other wisemen."

The King insisted, "I know, but you are the best wiseman

in this area. I command you to accept. If you refuse, your career will be ruined, and you will be beheaded. Besides, the job pays 100 pence more a day." Ernie humbly accepted and took over the serfdom.

After a year or two of lessons hard learned, Ernie's skills as a supervisor grew and eventually he became known throughout the land as a chief of wisemen, only to be rivaled by Morris. And they lived happily ever after.

This fairy tale is true, for it is the account of how this author moved into his supervisory role. It is also an accurate reflection of how many people in the mental health field, and in particular the substance abuse field, move into supervisory positions. Unlike in business, health care delivery personnel move quickly up the ranks to supervisory positions. With the rapid growth of service delivery agencies in the 1970s, many counselors found themselves being promoted into decision-making positions soon after their entry into the field. Individuals found themselves overwhelmed with the responsibilities of the job. Many had little or no experience or training in management and supervisory skills. Many had not been exposed to clinical supervision themselves.

Currently, supervisors are often made in the substance abuse field by being in the right place at the right time. One becomes a supervisor quickly and by chance. This contributes to the significantly high turnover rate and career growth potential in service delivery agencies today.

It is assumed that once a counselor has "learned the trade," he is automatically qualified to teach it and to supervise others. Yet, if certain skills are necessary to practice counseling, which can be learned either in a formal academic setting or through life experiences, it seems reasonable to think that one could also learn to be a clinical supervisor. A good counselor is not necessarily a good supervisor. Supervisory skills should be explicitly taught. Clinical supervision is more than simply teaching someone 150 ways to say "ah ha." On the other hand, a good supervisor must himself be a good counselor. Although some have had supervisory training, the vast majority have not had this opportunity.

This is further complicated by the confusion over what exactly is clinical supervision. Some claim to have been supervisors for years when in fact they misunderstand the meaning of the term. The definition used in this book for the term "clinical supervision" is that it is a "disciplined tutorial process wherein principles are transformed into practical skills" (Rapoport, 1954). Around this simple definition, more complex understandings of the term will be developed in the text.

It is time that the substance abuse and mental health fields "come of age" by refining the skills of supervisors and providing more thorough training in the decision-making role in an agency. There should be the development of a cadre with clinical supervisory skills, able to provide appropriate and adequate clinical training to individuals. This has not as yet occurred in the substance abuse field. It involves helping people to conceptualize, analyze, and improve their supervisory skills, relationships, techniques, and interventions. These supervisors must be helped to establish a comprehensive system of case management for health care facilities. Finally, the level of in-service training provided to counselors must be upgraded so eventually a self-perpetuating system for counselor skill development and clinical supervisory training will have been devised.

To do this, the field must develop a philosophy and sound conceptual scheme of both clinical and administrative supervision so that individuals in supervisory positions can develop a repertoire of supervisory interactions.

In the fairy tale, two things made it possible for Ernie to function as a supervisor of wisemen: his wise sayings and counseling abilities, and his own experience under Morris' supervision. These are the prerequisities for being a clinical supervisor. The other competencies and skills can be learned. This book will provide the background to the skills necessary to function as a clinical supervisor in the mental health field.

Throughout the book the terms alcohol abuse, alcoholism, drug addiction, and substance abuse will be used interchangeably. Further, although the book will focus upon substance abuse counselors, the principles for clinical supervisors are transferable to those in all health care delivery systems, including mental health counselors, social service professionals, motivational and referral counselors, etc.

Finally, in the interest of unisexism, "he" and "she" will be used interchangeably to refer to the counselor and/or supervisor.

Chapter 1

THE STATE OF THE ART OF TRAINING

EAAETP NEEDS ASSESSMENT SURVEY

Since 1970, the alcoholism and drug abuse fields have experienced an incredible growth in the number and range of educational programs available to counselors. Colleges and universities have "jumped on the bandwagon" in developing degree-level training programs. Summer institutes for studies on alcoholism have cropped up in most states with what appears to be a never-ending supply of attendees. There has been an explosion and proliferation in the number of curriculum guides, short-term courses, workshops, seminars, and conferences for counselors. In fact, the field may be in danger of glutting the market with energetic, committed, trained, and unemployed counselors. Leaders in the field must carefully examine the present needs and priorities in education and training so that appropriate short- and long-term manpower planning may occur.

In 1975, the Eastern Area Alcohol Education and Training Program, Inc. (EAAETP) conducted a comprehensive needs assessment survey of education priorities in 16 eastern states. The study involved interviews with 514 training and treatment program directors, 450 individuals who have attended training programs in the past five years, 16 state alcoholism and drug abuse authorities, and various "grassroots" level counselors. The following are the findings of that needs assessment survey. In the light of the results of other needs assessment studies, these findings appear to be reflective of the national training picture.

Of 60 educational centers surveyed by the EAAETP, major funding sources for programs appeared to be state formula grant monies and tuitions. The average number of trainees per program was 90, with the mean number of days of training being 13. Over two-thirds of the programs required no minimum period of sobriety for admission, and 96.4 percent required no prior experience in the substance abuse field as a prerequisite for admission. Only 28.6 percent of the training programs provided field experience or client contact to trainees; 78 percent of the programs provided either certificates of completion or no other form of trainee recognition, such as continuing education units, and undergraduate or graduate credits.

Graduates of these training programs felt they learned the least in clinical skills, such as individual, family, and group counseling techniques; crisis intervention counseling skills; client outcome evaluation methodology; and assessment methods. Adequate exposure seems to be provided to trainees in the basics on alcohol, alcoholism, and drug abuse. However, it was the area of advanced skill building that trainees complained they were getting the least training.

The preferred method of training was on-the-job training, workshops, and field placement and observations, involving clinical experiences. Through "learning by doing" trainees might receive more practical information which they could relate to their own work experiences.

The overall "state of the art" of training appears to be most spotty, unplanned, uncoordinated, and duplicative, with a proliferation of efforts which may be meeting the needs of trainers more than the needs of trainees. Prospective trainees are left with a confusing array of schools, institutes, and workshops presenting attractive titles but which may not in the long-run be making any measurable impact upon the skills of the counselors. Many may simply be providing attendees with a mecca of training, hearing a big name speaker, or exchanged names and addresses (and if fortunate, ideas) informally with others after the sessions, but little substantive help.

Summer institutes and workshops play a central role in the initial entry level education of caregivers, providing basic information about the nature and extent of substance abuse, and introductory skills on counseling. However, additional training experiences must be provided. Counselors often find themselves "charged up" after their initial training experiences only to become bewildered and panic-stricken after several months on the job. They realize that they still know little about conducting individual, family, and group counseling sessions. Many draw upon their own life experiences, either in therapy or in Twelve-Step work in AA. But they soon realize that this is insufficient preparation for dealing with the complex range of problems encountered in counseling.

Training programs have also failed to provide adequate recognition to graduates, to relate curriculum to the competencies necessary to function, to provide practicum experiences so trainees can "learn by doing," and, to provide skill development training rather than educational experiences.

Training programs have not adequately taken into account the major obstacles and needs of adult trainees, which are

The costs involved in residential training (travel, per diem, tuition, etc.)

The length of training sessions which leaves the employer short-staffed

The hardships on trainees being away from home and work for extended periods

The needs of counselors to develop their own self-identity through peer and colleague evaluations

These limitations have not adequately been considered in the development of training programs for counselors. The characteristics of the adult learning experience have also not adequately been considered in developing a sound educational experience. Counselors tend to be laypersons without formal academic training which perpares them for their positions. The supervisors of these counselors may not be counselors themselves, but may be program administrators with limited clinical supervisory experience. On the other hand, counselors are motivated to improve their skills and to be prepared for credentialling. Agencies are interested in upgrading the level of skills of their counselors so that quality care can be provided and agency accreditation may be established.

Missing Puzzle Pieces

Several of the necessary pieces to the confusing training puzzle are presently available: summer/winter schools and institutes, short-term seminars and conferences, intensive training programs, and academic degree programs, both in undergraduate and graduate levels. Recently, there has been a rapid growth in the number of summer/winter schools, each state feeling the need to have its own institute that is bigger and better than the others. Efforts have been made to consolidate these schools on a regional basis. However, additional efforts must be expended in finding the commonalities in the programs and establishing ground rules for any further proliferation of summer/winter institutes.

The number of short-term conferences and workshops is

mind-boggling. The EAAETP publishes a bi-monthly bulletin of alcoholism conferences in the 16 eastern states. The *Information Bulletin* includes nearly 30 entries per issue. Yet this is not inclusive of all the sessions conducted in the east. By multiplying that number nationally, it could be conservatively estimated that there are in excess of 200 seminars and conferences on alcoholism alone conducted every two months.

Considerable planning should be devoted to standardizing these programs and establishing guidelines for short-term conferences. The rule of thumb presently is "let the buyer beware" for the quality of short-term workshops varies greatly. A number of "trainers" in these conferences realize the money-making potential of short-term workshops. Quality has been sacrificed for marketing value, for what will draw participants, and how high a fee the market will bear.

The number and quality of intensive training programs has grown also in the past five years. These might be defined as training courses of intermediate duration (4 to 26 weeks) often residential and involving practicum experiences. Examples of such programs might be the Regional Training Programs of Johns Hopkins University (a six-week residential session and an eighteen-week field placement experience), or the Dartmouth Counselor Training Program (a four-week residential course with practicum experience additional).

Although the quality of training at most intensive programs is excellent, the time and financial restraints are inconsistent with meeting the needs of the employed counselor.

The last puzzle piece presently in place is that of academic degree programs at the undergraduate and graduate levels. Many of the newly developed programs claim to have competency-based curricula. However, many of the programs resort to providing trainees only field observation experiences, with minimal client contact. It will be necessary in the future for academically-based training programs to provide a modularized curriculum geared to the employed counselor who can only attend on a part-time basis.

Several puzzle pieces have to be added to provide a comprehensive planned approach to training, offering a diverse range of educational opportunities to meet the specific needs of counselors at the various stages of their professional development (Fig 1). These pieces are:

Competency-based testing mechanisms
Development of a cadre of trainers
Quality in-service training programs
Accreditation of counselor training programs
Advanced clinical training programs
Clinical supervision

The first step in developing a curriculum for counselor training ought to be outlining the specific goals and objectives for courses and the competencies which graduates are expected

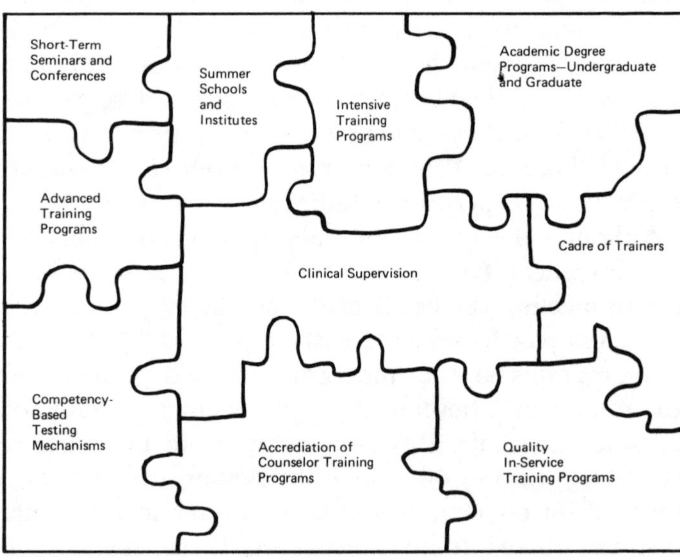

Fig. 1. The confusing puzzle of counselor training programs.

to acquire. This step is often avoided by training programs. It involves establishing baselines on the skills necessary for counselors to function, outlining the tasks to be performed, and the competencies needed to fulfill those tasks. Tasks and competencies should be organized into defined curriculum modules for training purposes. (Tasks in this context mean the cluster of work functions that form a specific intervention which may either be therapeutic or administrative.) Competencies are defined as the knowledge base and skills required to perform a particular task.

The problem in establishing a competency-based curriculum is that of monitoring and evaluating the competencies acquired by trainees. As yet, the state of the art of training has not reached a stage in which objective testing of clinical competencies is readily attained. The subjective judgments of the clinical supervisor and trainer remains the most valid evaluation of clinical competencies. Although considerable effort is underway to develop competency-based testing mechanisms, some distance still must be traveled before quantitative clinical skills evaluations can be made. The second piece of the puzzle presently is that of a cadre of trainers categorized by the areas in which they are skilled at training. Categorization efforts must be linked to a national training network and classification system. Eventually, it will be necessary to credential trainers.

The third element presently missing is the improvement of in-service training programs for the staff of treatment agencies. Chapter 10 of the book will address this issue.

The fourth piece of the puzzle is that of accrediting counselor training programs. Standards must be established on a regional and national basis. EAAETP has begun this process by accrediting training programs in the 16 eastern states, which should be linked to a national accrediting body. Baselines should be established as to what constitutes approved training. Accreditation of training programs is the most efficient and cost effective mechanism for this purpose.

Fifth, advanced clinical training programs must be expanded to allow for more trainees. Presently, trainee slots in these programs are limited.

Lastly, the most important piece in the clinical training picture is that of clinical supervision. The justification for this element will be discussed in subsequent pages. Throughout the book the term "clinical supervision" will be used to mean an intensive one-to-one or small group experience in which an "apprentice" in the field discusses with a "master" clinical situations and issues. Staff development refers to all agency procedures that enhance the job-related knowledge and skills of its staff, such as training sessions, lectures, workshops, conferences, readings, discussion groups, etc. In-service training is a specific form of staff development for a delimited staff group. In-service becomes a generalized learning context for issues that might be raised in clinical supervision. Thus, the two are complementary.

Clinical supervision refers to a specific aspect of staff development dealing with the clinical skills and competencies of staff, including problems encountered and individual needs. The supervisor focuses upon what the counselor needs to know to deliver treatment services to specific clients. The conselor can thus move from knowing to doing. The supervisor ensures that the staff will develop professionally and personally.

Clinical supervision makes a significant impact upon counselors. It is the most advanced, threatening, and challenging form of clinical training. It is also a prerequisite for the maintenance of quality health care. To not utilize the problem-solving techniques of clinical supervision is to believe in magic, that conflicts, inadequacies, and problems will go away by themselves. It is similar to one wishing he could lose weight and believing in the "fat fairy" who comes at night and takes away all ugly fat.

Chapter 2

WHY CLINICAL SUPERVISION?

Questions can be raised, "If the pieces of the puzzle are in place or will be implemented shortly, why is clinical supervision so important? Will counselors not be adequately trained in other programs? Will clinical supervision not be provided in these training programs at field placement sites? Is the added administrative and financial burden necessary?"

These questions assume that learning is a static, one-time occurrence, embodied in a specific curriculum. However, adult learning theory has demonstrated that optimal learning occurs over an extended period of time with constant reinforcements and re-examinations of one's knowledge and skills.

In the minds of many, education is primarily concerned with abstract concepts, and associated with textbooks and academic processes. The classroom symbolizes the assumption that education is a specific activity cut off from the real world and unrelated to one's life. Research, though, has demonstrated that classroom performance (grades) has little correlation with one's success or failure in later life. It is because of these assumptions that learning is seldom seen as important or relevant in later life. Hence, the adult counselor resists the process of education.

The substance abuse counselor is typically an older individual with a varied background of life experiences and formal training. Some may have struggled with their own abusive use of alcohol and/or other drugs. Adult learning for such an individual is extremely important, but the trainer must take into account how the counselor learns. This involves a cyclical, problem-solving process of four stages as reflected in Figure 2.

This learning process is governed by the person's needs, goals, learning styles, and experiences. Adult learning must be individualized to the needs of each trainee. The optimal learning picture for the nondegreed counselor includes repeated opportunities for evaluation, critiquing, and relearning. Without clinical supervision, training programs, although all necessary and valuable in and of themselves, fall short of ultimately providing a finished counselor with optimal professional skills and competencies.

Clinical supervision meets a number of needs as outlined in the following paragraphs.

1. Supervision is an intensive learning experience providing counselors feedback on and assessment of their

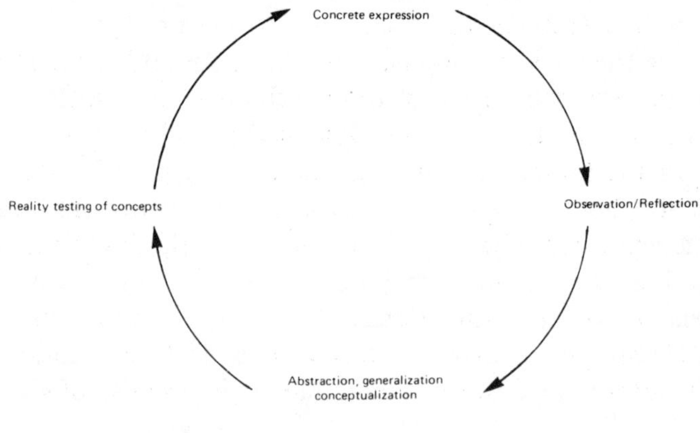

clinical skills. Studies have indicated the expressed need of counselors for this feedback.

The quality of supervision directly impacts on job satisfaction, turnover, and ultimately, service delivery. While research within the substance abuse field is limited, general mental health manpower studies have indicated the importance of supervision. Henry, Sims, and Spray (1971), based on a sample of over 1000 psychiatric social workers, reported that clinical supervision was the most important training experience for those surveyed. Miller (1970) examined the job satisfaction of entry level social workers and found that the supervisor's technical incompetence was one of the most frequent sources of dissatisfaction among the staff. These findings were replicated in studies of Kermish and Kushin, (1969). Workers in state rehabilitation programs were studied by Aiken, Smits, and Lollar, (1972). It was found that the clinical supervisory relationship was the most satisfying component of their job. It was more important to the workers than the conditions on the job or the organization's reward system. Olmstead and Christensen (1973) demonstrated that high scores on the quality of clinical supervision correlated with greater job satisfaction, less absenteeism, better inidvidual and agency performance, and higher skill levels of staff.

2. Kadushin, (1973) pointed out a number of sources of satisfaction that counselors derive from clinical supervision:

Emotional support is provided to counselors.

Clinical responsibilities are shared.

A resource person is available to discuss client behavior.

Professional development is enhanced.

Discussion of the theory and practice of counseling is stimulated.

Critical feedback is provided.

An appreciation for the employing agency and a sense of belonging is conveyed.

A forum for personal growth is provided.

Supervision constitutes a key factor in the effective and efficient delivery of quality treatment services. It is especially important in the substance abuse field where counselors are constantly confronted with the despair, frustration, and denial of clients. Supervision provides a mechanism for reduction in counselor "burn-out," a problem that is most significant in the alcoholism and drug abuse fields.

3. Counselors must deal with emotionally latent content that drains emotional energy. The range of problems dealt with—parent-child relationships, physical illness, death, marital conflicts, physical abuse, deviance, sexual behavior—are problems everyone confronts at some point in life. Counseling responsibilities are great; the risks for creating stress, anxiety, guilt, frustration, voyeurism, and unconscious reactions in the counselor are significant. Clinical supervision is an important way of assisting the counselor in dealing with the demands of the clinical world.

   Students under supervision most often prize personal growth over professional growth in their training. However, personal growth ultimately leads to behavioral changes and increased clinical competence. They acquire self-confidence, a sense of self as counselor, and increased comfort and proficiency in counseling situations.
4. Indirectly, clinical supervision impacts on the quality of health care provided to clients. On the other hand, inadequate supervision can detract from service delivery. For example, client care is impaired if a supervisor

does not aid the counselor in formulating diagnostic and psychotherapeutic competencies. Ineffective supervision serves to demotivate counselors, break down a team concept, and add to overall job dissatisfaction, all of which impact on the quality of care. Inadequate supervision contaminates the work milieu through inhibiting organizational goal setting.

5. Supervision provides an internal monitoring and evaluation mechanism, or a thermometer to measure ourselves. Information about the counselor's skills is offered. Quality control mechanisms are provided to training institutions as to the acquired skills of graduates and areas in which curricula can be improved. The nature of counseling prohibits direct observation of counselors on a daily basis. Staff is protected from direct scrutiny. Supervision provides a monitoring system of the quality of agency care.

    In contrast with other professions where personnel behavior is observable and measurable, such as the work of a surgeon, the causal relationship between the actions of a counselor and client is not necessarily clear. Supervision is one of the few methods for guarding against poor counseling. In the alcoholism field, with the absence of a peer monitoring and utilization review system, such as a Professional Services Review Organization (PSRO), clinical supervison is essential.

6. Staffing is an important managerial function for the employer, involving hiring, training, evaluating, promoting, disciplining, and firing employees. In fulfilling these tasks, the supervisor is aided in larger agencies by the services of a personnel department. Yet, the supervisor is the key figure in the staffing functions, for she alone is in a position to evaluate job performance. In health care agencies, performance evaluation is most difficult unless supervision is provided. A staff member basically has to sleep with the the boss' wife

or punch a client to require disciplinary action. Without a constant feedback mechanism, a supervisor does not have the necessary information and documentation to take administrative action when needed.

The author recalls a counselor under his employ who seemed to be doing adequate work. However, there were rumors of unethical and unprofessional counseling practices occurring. Because this counselor was inadequately supervised there were no grounds for disciplinary action. It was not until weekly, and at times, daily, clinical supervision was provided that it became possible to take action. Thus, clinical supervision is necessary as a personnel management procedure.

7. Finally, an agency has a legal and ethical responsibility to the clients to provide adequate staff supervision. Malpractice suits continue to accelerate; the Joint Commission on the Accreditation of Hospitals continues to review facilities. Clinical supervision is becoming an important policing mechanism on agency professionalism.

Counseling is an amorphous process, difficult to evaluate and distinguish what constitutes ethical practice. However, accreditation of facilities and credentialling of counselors necessitate a system for evaluating staff skills and functioning. Further, as counselor certification standards continue to move closer towards competency-based models, the subjective judgments of supervisors are crucial in evaluating counselor skills. It provides checks on staff behavior in a field in which nonuniform tasks are performed in uncertain contexts, towards the accomplishment of ambiguous and diffuse goals with a heterogeneous population.

In sum, clinical supervision is an important ingredient in the puzzle of counselor training. Agencies must begin to develop their own clinical supervisory systems.

Number hrs/wk clinical supervision	*Me. N=20*	*N.H. N=20*	*Vt. N=29*	*Mass. N=55*	*R.I. N=19*	*Conn. N=35*	*N.Y. N=60*	*N.J. N=27*	*Del. N=25*	*Pa. N=53*	*Va. N=57*	*Md. N=45*	*W.V. N=42*	*D.C. N=12*	*P.R. N=9*	*V.I. N=6*
None	40%	61.5%	66.4%	45.9%	57.2%	72%	57.5%	41.3%	55%	38.2%	61%	26.5%	66.4%	40%	28.6%	100%
1–2	33.3%	38.5%	16.8%	48.5%	28.6%	28%	31.9%	43.8%	20%	34.4%	29.3%	42.0%	20.6%	15%	71.4%	0
3–5	20%	0	8.4%	2.8%	14.2%	0	10.6%	8.9%	20%	20.6%	7.3%	22.6%	10.4%	40%	0	0
6 or more	6.7%	0	8.4%	2.8%	0	0	0	6.0%	5%	6.8%	0	8.9%	2.6%	5%	0	0

From Powell, David J. *Manpower needs in the alcohol field.* Bloomfield, Conn.: EAAETP, Inc., 1976, p. 175.

Fig. 3. State by State Analysis of Intramural Training Efforts in the Agencies Interviewed (N = 514).

In the substance abuse field, however, there is a sparsity of supervision being provided. *Manpower Needs in the Alcohol Field* reports that 49.8 percent of the study's respondents stated that they received no clinical supervision. Of those supervised, another 8 percent stated that they were provided supervision by a nondegreed counselor with no prior experience under clinical supervision.

These figures are substantiated by a study conducted by the Medical College of Pennsylvania in 1976 which found that only a small percentage of their trainees over the past three years were provided clinical supervision after the completion of training. Also, both studies found a disturbing absence of training for supervisors. Although attention is given to supervisory techniques in graduate programs, supervision is by no means universally addressed in training programs. Further, many supervisors in the substance abuse field do not hold graduate degrees and thus would not have an opportunity to receive either clinical supervisory training or experience under supervision.

In summary, although a number of education and training puzzle pieces are presently in place, other components have yet to be realized, most importantly, clinical supervision. This last piece will be the most endearing and productive component of counselor training for it directly impacts upon the quality of care provided to clients. Without supervision, the puzzle remains incomplete and the field continues to struggle outside of the mainstream of the mental health field, with inadequately trained and evaluated counselors possessing limited skills and competencies.

Chapter 3

WHAT IS CLINICAL SUPERVISION?

DIMENSIONS OF SUPERVISION (Fig. 4)

Supervision literally means "super" or "over" and "videre" or "to watch, to see." Webster's New Collegiate Dictionary (1975) defines a supervisor as an "overseer, one who watches over the work of another with responsibility for its quality." It is also, however, an educational process in which a person with expertise and skill takes responsibility for training another person with less background and competency. The dimensions of supervision are far broader than those associated solely with administrative functions.

The job of supervisor in a health care facility is a demanding one. It involves four major dimensions. First, a supervisor must be a good *boss* and *manager.* He must have the technical, professional, and clinical skills to run the program smoothly and to see that the staff carries out their responsibilities successfully. It is expected that the clinical supervisor has a grasp of the key theoretical concepts of counseling, such as differential

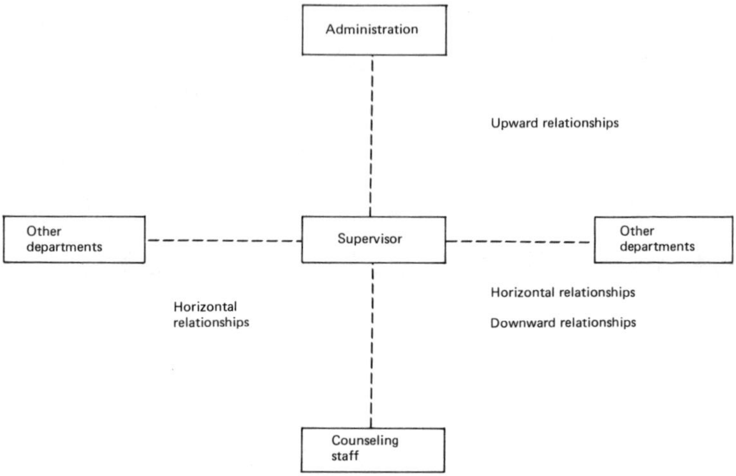

Fig. 4. Dimensions of supervision.

diagnosis, transference, countertransference, developmental and personality theory, therapeutic change processes, etc.

Second, the supervisor must be a competent *subordinate* to the decision makers above her. In many instances in the small agencies, the middle supervisor also represents top management, reporting only to a board of directors or advisory council. Many agencies are isolated without an involved hierarchical structure and an overall program administrator responsible for the management of the program. However, it is necessary that the supervisor maintain good employer/employee relationships with his superiors.

The third supervisory dimension is as a *connecting link* between employees and the administration. To employees, the supervisor represents the program's administration who can take disciplinary action when needed. This can create problems and resistances towards the clinical supervisor. Thus, the clinical supervisor is that part of the administration who must make certain that the clinical operations of the program are being performed in a professional and ethical manner.

The fourth dimension of the supervisor's role is that she

must maintain satisfactory relationships with intra- and extramural providers. In large health care facilities, such as hospitals, this involves relating to other department heads. These relationships must be that of a *good colleague,* willing and eager to coordinate her program's efforts with others in order to reach common goals.

The clinical supervisor must be successful in the vertical relationships downward with staff and upward with superiors. In addition, he must be skillful in facilitating horizontal relationships with other professionals.

In addition to their many obligations, supervisors also "wear the hats" of:

- providing direct patient care themselves
- being liaisons with other staff
- delegating authority for the care of patients
- planning, directing, and controlling all activities of the unit
- making rounds at medical facilities
- personal observation of the condition and behavior of clients
- assessing the needs of the unit for continuing care
- interpreting and applying the policies, procedures, and rules of the program
- orienting new personnel and acquainting individuals with the philosophies of the program
- continuing in-service education and other training responsibilities
- personnel monitoring and evaluation
- coordinating patient care with other programs
- designing and regulating the fiscal aspects of the unit
- attending professional meetings, conferences, and symposia, etc., as a representative of that program

It is exhausting just reading through this list. One wonders what the supervisor does in his free time? The job of supervisor is a demanding and challenging one.

All of these tasks, though, can be simplified into two main dimensions: (1) The supervisor must have a thorough knowledge of the tasks to be performed, possess the technical and clinical competencies to do that job, and be able to convey this knowledge to others. (2) She must be a manager for that program. As a manager, the supervisor becomes a special person in the organization as the analyzer and developer for the program. Since she is in a higher position in organizational hierarchy than others, she can design, review, and enforce the decisions of the agency. She has the power and authority (at least in most agencies) to do so. She has the responsibility of inspecting the work of the staff and of developing and initiating programs to intervene and remedy job performance problems.

The key, though, to these supervisory dimensions is that the "product" in a health care agency is "people." One must never lose sight of that. Supervisors are in the business to help others, not solely to maintain jobs for the money or status. The supervisor in an alcoholism program faces all of the demands on his time that a manager in business encounters plus the added responsibility of dealing with the lives of others. Errors in this program do not just result in drop-offs in profits, productivity, or the number of chickens cooked each day. It results in an impact upon human lives. All are guilty at times of forgetting that the business is people-oriented. Thus, the overriding dimension for the supervisor is that he must be concerned for clients and not production.

The supervisor is involved in the personal and professional growth of the counselor and the emotional, physical, and psychological health of the client. Supervision becomes a cooperative educational process wherein the supervisor aids the staff in achieving better client care.

In accordance with this dual goal, the relationship between supervisor and counselor resembles a mixture of an apprenticeship and a form of psychotherapy. The supervisor is skilled in his discipline, that expertise is transmitted via an apprenticeship. In so far as the supervision is directed towards the counselor's personal growth, it bears a strong resemblance to the psychotherapeutic relationship.

The supervisor also provides an expressive-supportive function for staff by promoting morale, helping with job-related discouragements and discontentments, and helping with the development of a sense of professionalism, belonging, and security. To do this, the supervisor utilizes procedures such as reassurance, recognition of achievement, encouragement, expressions of confidence, praise, approval, ventilation, catharsis, and listening to the concerns of the staff. This supportive function is complementary to the educational and administrative aspects of supervision since the ultimate goal of the functions is the delivery of quality care.

Ekstein and Wallerstein (1972) portray the clinical nature of the supervisory relation in what is termed "a clinical rhombus" which connects the four components of a clinical system: therapist, administration, patient, and supervisor (Fig. 5). These four components are connected in a fluid rather than a fixed relationship. This is what distinguishes clinical from administrative supervision.

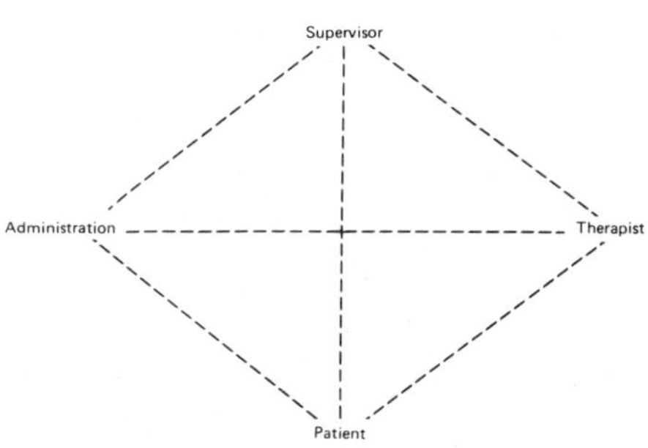

Fig. 5. A clinical rhombus. From Ekstein & Wallenstein, *The teaching and learning of psychotherapy,* 2nd ed. New York: International Universities Press, 1972.

The Needs of Counselors, Clients, and Agencies

Counselor Needs

Each staff member is motivated by a number of needs, some of which may be unsatisfied. These unmet needs cause her to behave in a certain manner. Simply stated, we eat because we are hungry. We seek to achieve because we need reward and approval. A counselor can become overinvolved with a client because of her underlying need for success, in which case, the needs-fulfillment becomes destructive (Fig. 6). It is important for the supervisor to examine the various personal and professional needs of the staff in a relationship of trust, warmth, openness, and honest collaboration. Active conflict and professional growth should be facilitated.

Abraham Maslow (1970) has formed a theory of needs fulfillment based on a hierarchy of needs (Fig. 7). Maslow's model contains five levels of needs that can be visualized as forming a pyramid. The lower order of needs are *physiological,* of a biological nature that everyone has for food, shelter, rest, and recreation. Normally, the counselor's paycheck provides the vitals to meet these needs. However, the salary range for

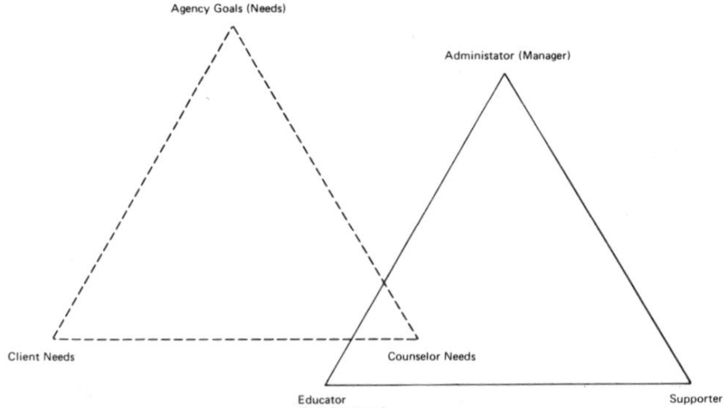

Fig. 6. Matching clinical supervisory roles to needs.

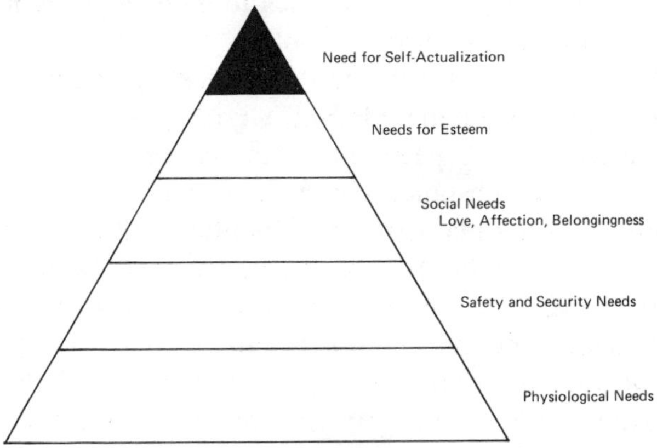

Fig. 7. Maslow's model of human needs.

many counselors is notably low, in the range of $8000 to 10,000; thus, some of the basic physiological needs may be unmet. It is essential for a supervisor to examine this most basic of staff needs to see if it is being adequately met.

When physiological needs are reasonably satisfied, the next higher level of needs begin to motivate the individual: *safety needs.* Everyone desires more control and protection over the uncertainties of life. Arbitrary management action is feared, such as loss of job, favoritism, discrimination, unpredictable administration of policy, etc. This is especially relevant in the substance abuse field which lives "hand to mouth" with federal and state dollars, dependent year to year on the whims of the bureaucracy. There is a significant turnover rate in the field, and very often unstable employment situations. Thus, this is a central need to be examined in the field for it may create stress and anxiety for staff.

Third, *social needs* become important behavioral motivators, consisting of the need for belonging, association, acceptance by peers, giving and receiving friendships, and approval.

Deprivation of this need produces role-playing and seductive behavior as the counselor tries to gain the affection of others. He seeks out an affirmation of his worthiness. Social needs are often identical with the need for a feeling of group identity, for being part of or included in a group, being accepted and respected by one's peers and fellow-workers.

In the substance abuse field, counselors find themselves outside of the mainstream of mental health workers, alienated by the nature of their work, unaccepted as an equal professional. Many counselors are lay-persons with limited formal academic training; there is a sense of not belonging to related professional groups, such as social work or psychological associations. To compensate for this, alcoholism counselors are forming their own peer groups to provide some degree of acceptance and identity.

A supervisor must be aware of these needs and hopefully will allow counselors to be fulfilled by the organization's informal groupings. Tightly knit, cohesive work groups generally enable counselors to gain greater on-the-job satisfaction and produce a better climate for motivation. There is, however, by the nature of the counseling field, a "lone ranger" image. Counselors feel like mini-magicians with their own bag of tricks used to weave their magic. Counseling is performed for the most part as a solitary act between client and staff. The functions of the counselor do not allow for social needs to be satisfied. The role of the supervisor is crucial in providing opportunities for group acceptance and respectability among peers.

After the social needs comes the *need for self-esteem.* Self-esteem includes the needs for self-confidence, independence, competence, achievement, knowledge, etc. Also involved are needs for influence, power, respect, control, and admiration. These needs can be fulfilled by knowing inside oneself that he can fulfill a task. However, counselors rarely get feedback on whether the tasks were properly accomplished. Self-evaluations are made in terms of failures more so than by successes. Someone must communicate to the counselor that she is successful and is appropriately performing the tasks.

Counselors also need to have recognition from others for their accomplishments, such as the gaining of reputation, status, appreciation, and the deserved respect of colleagues. To win that respect, counselors frantically rush after meaningless pieces of paper stating they have attended various schools or workshops. Credentialling of counselors is a step towards providing them with a sense of acceptability.

The clinical supervisor must take into account the staff's social needs if she is to be able to adequately provide further skill development training. If social needs continue to be unmet, the counselor may intentionally or unconsciously use the patient to enhance her needs through manipulations, authoritarian pressuring, belittling, mocking, attacking, seduction, preaching, etc. The counselor may become very task-oriented, using "dime store" psychology with clients. These behaviors can be destructive and should be avoided.

The highest level of needs is *self-actualization/self-fulfillment,* "to become what one is capable of becoming." Unlike the other four needs, self-actualization is seldom fully achieved. Conditions of modern life give little opportunity for one to fulfill their needs. Most counselors continuously struggle to satisfy lower needs and must divert their energies to them. Therefore the need for self-fulfillment frequently remains unfulfilled.

There is a relationship between the hierarchy of needs and age. When a counselor reaches adulthood, the needs of childhood fade and esteem seems to dominate his life. If he is successful, then he may be able to move on to self-actualization. The supervisor must aid staff in satisfying the lower needs so the counselor can reach the self-realized stage of development. The supervisor can assist in alleviating blockages that prohibit that growth process.

The supervisor must examine carefully the relationship of

age to counselor needs. EAAETP's needs assessment indicated that the majority of counselors are older (mean age of 39) with a background of other careers prior to their entry into the field, and often with a history of alcoholism (in the case of EAAETP) themselves. These factors must be taken into account if the supervisor is to aid staff in their professional development and skill training, (see Tables 1 and 2).

The counselor brings with him a range of experiences and attitudes developed through his response to reality. These must be accounted for by the clinical supervisor. Counselors are likely to have been out of school for some time. They are less

Table 1. Breakdowns of the Periods of Sobriety*

Number of years sober (N = 171)	*Percentage*
Years (N = 171)	
0–1	2.0
1–2	11.0
3–4	28.0
5–6	15.5
7–8	10.5
9–10	6.5
11–12	6.5
13–15	4.0
16–20	12.0
21 or more	4.0
Age (N = 450)	
21–25	7.8
26–30	22.0
31–35	12.5
36–40	15.3
41–45	11.1
46–50	12.7
51–55	9.0
56–60	3.6
61–65	3.4
66 or older	2.2
No response	0.4

*Of those individuals that classified themselves as recovered or recovering alcoholics (38.2%) the median number of years of sobriety was 5.9 years.

Table 2. Number of Years of Salaried Employment in the Field of Alcoholism (N = 450)

Years	*Percentage*
0–1	13.4
1–2	39.0
3–4	25.6
5–6	9.5
7–8	3.9
9–10	3.6
11–12	1.4
13–14	0.6
15–16	0.3
17–18	1.1
19–20	0.6
20 or more	1.0

likely to have well-habituated formal study patterns and less recent practice in reading, note-taking, and paper-writing procedures. Further, counselors' jobs are poorly defined and exist in agencies that are ambivalent about their status, and who may view the functions of the nondegreed counselor as being oriented mainly to such tasks as transporting patients, conducting recreational therapy programs, going to AA meetings with clients.

It is also important to examine the levels of counselor aspiration. Many staff are older and late achievers, and motivated for success and career growth. This can both aid or retard the growth process since counselors sometimes feel the need to make more demands upon themselves, to "push themselves." This behavior is especially observable in the recovering alcoholic.

Another factor is the attitudes of the staff. Attitudes constitute one's feelings about something, individual likes and dislikes directed towards persons, things, and situations. They are charged with overtones that include intellectual and emotional components. They have a direct impact upon client/counselor functioning. In classical terms, this might be called "countertransference."

Other factors contributing to attitude formation are age, sex, height, race, weight, physique, early childhood experiences, and environmental factors, such as education, employment, background, etc. The counselor is a mirror to himself of what he is or is not becoming. One should not forget that the broader culture also influences a person's attitudes. The United States believes that competition, reward for accomplishment, equal opportunities, nondiscrimination, etc., are part of the democratic, capitalist system. Individuals learn from an early age to strive for achievement, to think for themselves, to work hard. These are the roads to success.

However, in counseling, there are few opportunities to measure one's success, few indicators of accomplishment. Counselors go about their functioning without any approval or disapproval of what they are doing. This leads to anxiety and unfulfilled needs of acceptance so characteristic of the alcoholism counselor.

In sum, attitudes determine the route to satisfying needs. The same needs appear in everyone although individual attitudes may vary affecting one's unique responses to the needs. The clinical supervisor must carefully examine the staff members' needs. He must be aware of how these needs are fulfilled and how they impact upon the relationship of the counselor to clients. Many of these needs may not be apparent to the counselor. Yet, it is the supervisor's function to point out needs as he sees them in relation to how they affect counselor functioning.

If the supervisor fails to do this, unfulfilled needs can result in frustration and acting out by the counselor. There are a number of factors that contribute to the frustration: egoism of counselors; denial by clients and counselors; dependency relationships between staff and patients (the "good shepherd image" and "Messiah Complex"); client overloads; limitations on money, resources, and manpower; political situations and instability of most agencies; and, ambiguity of counselors' roles. Counselors deal with these frustrations in ways which may or may not be healthy and adaptive. Counselors may detour behavior and deny needs, or project problems onto others. They may also "burn-out" which is a retreat from the situation. Further, counselors may act out that frustration through aggressive behavior towards staff and/or clients. Sexual behavior is sometimes a form of such aggression. The most adaptive method, though, involves problem-solving behavior where the supervisor and counselors confront these frustrations and deal with the unsatisfied personal needs.

There seems to be a pattern to the first few years of counselor employment: They begin with a burning, missionary enthusiasm to "save" people, to help individuals through their life crises. Counselors are soon confronted, however, by their frustrating positions where they are viewed by other professionals as unskilled, unqualified, and poorly trained with limited abilities and capabilities. This leads to a stagnation stage where instead of realizing their dream of saving the world they are assigned to minimal patient care tasks. The frustration and stagnation is compounded by their poor salaries and status. He finds himself in a society where the physician is at the head and the counselor's hand are tied by the "medical hierarchial" schema. Rather than functioning as a member of a "round table society" with an equal voice in the treatment process, she is only another member of the harem serving at the will of the "sultan" (See Figure 8).

Finally, the counselor in utter frustration becomes apathetic. "Why should I care, no one else cares?" At this point, client care begins to show signs of the counselor's feelings. Clients begin to drop out of treatment. This may be excused as a lack of client motivation when, in fact, it results from counselor apathy.

The supervisor should support and educate the counselor through these troublesome days of employment.

Other clinical supervisor goals for personal growth and development are:

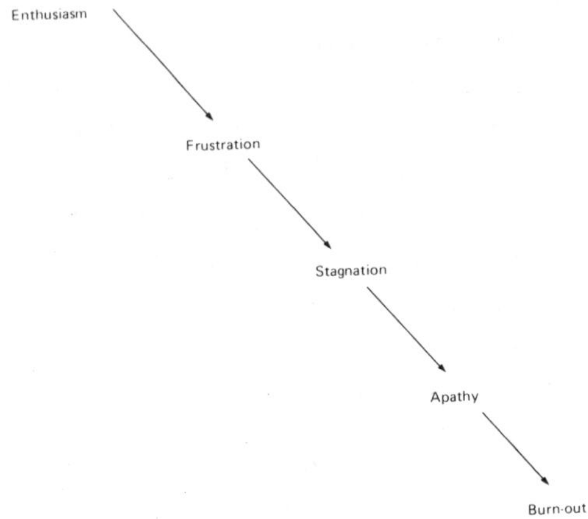

Fig. 8. A counselor's career.

1. An awareness of the counselor's interactions with others
2. Appropriate behavioral externalizations of feelings in proper places and times
3. A gradual blending of counselor goals and an incorporation of these goals into their daily life-styles
4. Honesty regarding intellectual and cognitive perceptions
5. Openness and receptivity to feedback
6. Willingness to try specific efforts to remedy areas of concern

To summarize, the clinical supervisor must deal with the personal and professional needs of staff. This involves a careful examination of the basic physical, psychological, and social needs of counselors, their stages of emotional development and maturity, and other factors, such as the counselor's age, sex, levels of aspiration, attitudes, biological and physiological make-up, environmental factors, and frustration tolerance.

This involves helping the counselor to explore blockages, anxieties, and countertransferences. This must always be done, however, in the context of the client, being respective of the counselor's own boundaries of privacy. While the supervisor helps the counselor to explore personal issues, the supervisor is not a substitute psychotherapist.

Client Needs

The supervisor plays a crucial role in assisting the counselor to understand the client's needs. In this sense the supervisor is an *educator* (teacher/skill developer) and a resource person to staff, capable of helping them learn what is needed for ongoing professional development.

As an educator, the supervisor may teach specific techniques of therapeutic intervention, such as reflection of feelings, group or family counseling techniques, reality therapy approaches, etc. She may teach basic interviewing skills, such as the importance of establishing client rapport or of not forcing a patient to relinquish symptoms. The supervisor may suggest theoretical positions which clarify client dynamics, or may familiarize the staff with predictable stages or crises in the therapeutic process.

In the educator role, the supervisor is removed from the client, and thus can assist the counselor in getting greater psychological distance. She may, for example, focus on the tone of the intervention instead of content, or provide feedback on specific clinical interactions and offer alternative approaches. The supervisor must be sensitive to changes in the counselor's style, or technique. Studies have pointed out that changes in the client often occur first in the awareness of the therapist and are only integrated by the client when reflected back to the patient by the counselor. The same process can occur in clinical supervision. The counselor may not notice when he has broken through a limitation for the first time. From a more objective vantage point the supervisor can point out the change and highlight the effects on the client.

The supervisor does not function in a vacuum: she is a coach attuned to the needs of each counselor. She knows the particular resources and vulnerabilities of the counselors and how these may contribute to or impede their functioning.

The supervisor should look for each counselor's particular strengths and then capitalize on the assets. Entry-level counselors often have narrow and rigid notions of the qualities that constitute therapeutic resources. In alcoholism counseling, the novice often has the concept that blatant confrontation is useful. However, the supervisor's familiarity with the discipline of counseling gives a greater appreciation for the actual diversity of therapeutic resources. Natural counseling strengths, such as humor, vivid imagery, or interpersonal warmth and strength can be modeled for staff by the supervisor. This aids counselors to appreciate the proper use of self in counseling. It also helps the new counselor with his inevitable doubts about his suitability for clinical work by reassuring him that he brings to the job therapeutic resources and qualities.

This point is crucial for the alcoholism supervisor whose staff probably consists of individuals with limited formal academic training and with self-doubts about their own therapeutic resources. "I know I am a good counselor because I did good Twelve-Step work. Well, at least I think I am. Aren't I?" The supervisor must point out the positive qualities of each counselor, such as empathy, genuineness, caring, etc. For the recovering alcoholic counselor, these are concrete resources that she possesses which often the formally trained individual may not have.

Further, the supervisor should point out the counselor's weaknesses in style. It is important to make clear to the novice counselor that no one is perfectly suited to clinical work, free from some quirk or nontherapeutic characteristic. All counselors have natural limitations. Competence does not eradicate all limitations but makes one aware of them and of their probable impact on clients. It involves the reduction of the potential for destructive behavior around those limitations.

The supervisor guides staff in a process of addressing weaknesses and limitations. For example, a counselor may have to practice dealing with clients' feelings instead of pulling clients back and forth with interrogations. Another counselor may need to learn about theoretical approaches to family systems. A third may need to explore her discomfort with older alcoholic clients. Some may need to work through these limitations by not dealing with certain types of clients. The supervisor may explore these options with the counselor and thereby help him develop a unique clinical style.

Nondegreed counselors often are not able to conceptualize and identify exactly what it is that they do with clients. Given their prior life experiences they deal with patients intuitively. The supervisor can aid in identifying what they are doing, naming that approach, and conceptualizing on why they do it. "So that's what they call what I do" is the response from counselors after this process. Thus, the supervisory relationship fosters trust, security, creativity, integration, and growth, attributes of the relationship that are crucial to the personal and professional growth of the counselor.

As the term "coach" implies, the supervisor may provide a pep talk to the staff to reassure them that they are acting appropriately and in a therapeutic manner. He may act as a model for the counselors in his own style of treatment, either by observation or by cotherapy. He may model a stance towards the discipline of counseling. Novice counselors are confronted with the complexity of human experiences. They are asked to understand and intervene therapeutically. The supervisor can provide a positive model on how to do this.

It has become increasingly chic in the substance abuse field to dismiss the knowledge and skills modeled by a supervisor and to plead intellectual poverty. "I just act out of my gut. Don't confuse me with academic junk." It is easy for the novice counselor to either clutch dogmatically at a simplistic approach, such as a party line Alcoholic Anonymous approach, or to cynically put down, in spite of her own anxiety, attempts to understand human development and pathology. The supervisor can aid counselors by modeling a stance combining conviction and skepticism. Ideally, the counselor should be free to think critically and independently within the clinical supervisory relationship. The supervisor can aid the counselor to see that theory and practice do mix, knowledge does not necessarily result in a decrease in one's concern for people.

The first step in meeting the needs of staff is for the clinical supervisor to establish baselines on the skills necessary for the counselor to function. A number of tasks whose effective accomplishment is essential in the delivery of quality services are necessary. Tasks refer to a cluster of work functions that jointly form a specific intervention (administrative or clinical). A series of competencies are then identified as part of the profile for each task. Competency is defined as the skills and knowledge needed to perform a particular task. Each competency profile includes a definition of the task, a range of various functions involved in that task, and competencies needed to effectively accomplish the task.

The specific tasks for substance abuse counselors have been outlined in credentialling standards, and include, but are not limited to, the following:

- intake and assessment
- assisting in developing a treatment plan
- individual, family, and group counseling
- continuous evaluation of client progress
- crisis intervention counseling
- follow-up contact, tracking, and referral
- seeking and using collateral support (employers, friends, etc.)
- reporting and record-keeping
- outreach

- case consultation
- identification of treatment gaps and overlaps
- assisting in program development
- identifying, mobilizing, and coordinating community resources
- education, prevention, and training
- program consultation

To perform these tasks, counselors must possess at least the following competencies. A clinical supervisor must discern the specific areas of need for each staff member. Certain counselors may be proficient in several areas but weak in others. It is the evaluative function of the supervisor to pick out the areas of strength and weakness, such as

- affective qualities, such as, empathy, concreteness, self-actualization, respect, genuineness, and congruence
- skills in assessing the stages of illness found in the client
- case history methodology skills
- skills in developing a treatment plan and in working through client reactions and resistances to this plan
- skills in making a referral should additional services be indicated
- ability to conceptualize on the therapeutic relationship
- ability to use counseling techniques to elicit feelings, facilitate understanding, and motivate the client
- ability to coordinate a client's continuum of treatment
- ability to participate in various inpatient and outpatient treatment processes; knowledge of their relationship, methods, and limitations
- ability to justify therapeutic interventions
- ability to maintain the necessary confidentiality safeguards

ability to maintain standards for ethical and professional practice

skills in assisting clients in recognizing and solving problems

ability to terminate a counseling session and a treatment plan

ability to prepare and conduct aftercare activities for the client

skills in maintaining client reports and records

This list is not intended to be exhaustive, although it probably is exhausting to the counselor who must have all of these skills. It is intended to be suggestive of the areas of strength and weakness that a counseling staff may have. It is the responsiblity of the clinical supervisor to assess each individual's area of need and to deal with these issues in supervisory sessions.

Agency Needs

The clinical supervisor is often an administrator/manager for the agency. She must meet the needs and demands of the program itself. The tasks of the supervisor as administrator include, but are not limited to, the following:

formulating organizational policies

public speaking on behalf of the agency

establishing operating budgets

controlling expenditures

contract negotiation

consulting with other professionals and agencies

program goal setting

fund raising and third party reimbursement negotiations

personnel and management practices and procedures

program evaluation, such as cost-effectiveness studies, research designs, analysis of data for program impact, treatment impact on clients

grantsmanship

formulating training methods and materials for the agency

staff screening, hiring, and evaluations

In the substance abuse field, little or no training is provided for supervisors in these areas. Most of what a supervisor does as an administrator is done because of his previous experiences in business or by chance.

Management is not a chance activity; it is the function of getting things done through other people, and directing the efforts of individuals towards a common objective. All of the above tasks can be condensed into five basic managerial functions: planning, organizing, staffing, influencing, and controlling (see Figure 9).

Planning is the function that determines in advance what programs that agency will conduct. It involves determining program goals, objectives, policies, procedures, and methods. In alcoholism agencies, managers often must fight one crisis after another. One month it might be an agency financial need; next month it might be a shortage of nursing staff or counselor overload. These problems are compounded by poor planning by managers. Also, although planning may be the first function that a manager must tackle, it does not stop when he goes on to the other functions. He continues to plan constantly while he performs his organizing, staffing, influencing, and controlling duties.

Organizing determines how the work of the agency will be divided and accomplished. In alcoholism programs organizing is essential given the limited number of staff and client overloads. It requires the manager to define, group, and assign job duties. To organize means to design a structural framework that outlines all the positions needed to perform the work of the

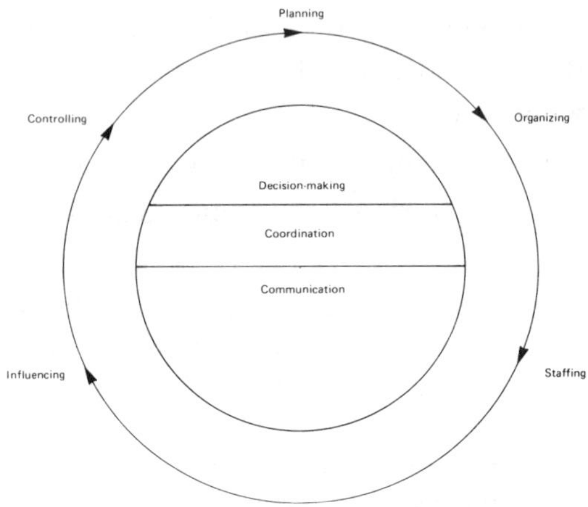

Fig. 9. Clinical supervisory functions.

agency and to assign responsibilities to these positions. It involves fitting this framework into the overall agency structure. This function also clarifies the lines of authority and responsibility within the program.

This framework is especially needed in outpatient treatment settings where there is a constant flow of clients. Group assignments, client caseloads, educational responsibilities, and tracking are dependent on a sound structural framework to assign staff. There must be a logical flow for people through the system. Because the supervisor must be aware of the client's status at every stage of care, tracking is essential.

The supervisor must also *staff* the program in keeping with the needs of the agency. Often alcoholism programs hire staff on the basis of the positions open and not on specific areas of programming need, nor the professional competencies needed by the program.

Staffing also includes the problems of promoting personnel in a field with limited career mobility and performance appraisal systems. The field is characterized by few objective job performance measurements and options for disciplinary action.

Influencing is concerned with motivating people to achieve agency objectives, and includes directing, guiding, teaching, coaching, and supervising. Obviously, there is an overlap with the clinical supervisory functions. In the managerial role, though, the supervisor is concerned primarily with the agency itself, its goals and objectives. It involves the personalizing of the planning, organizing, and staffing functions. It focuses on performance, productivity, leadership, and communication among staff and administration. It calls for interpreting the policies and procedures of the program to the counselors.

The managerial function of *control* involves ensuring that events proceed as planned and that objectives are achieved as developed: whether plans are being carried out, whether progress is being made towards the agency's objectives, what actions to take to correct any problems, etc. Control includes both taking corrective action if objectives are not being met, and revising plans and objectives if circumstances require.

Unfortunately, in health care facilities, the concept has developed that since the product is people, it is unnecessary for an agency to have measurable goals and objectives. The above management functions are not essential since there is only one purpose in being: to help people. Yet, every system must have clearly delineated statements of what the agency will accomplish, over what time frames and with what personnel.

It is helpful to think of these functions as a management cycle: a cycle is a system of interdependent processes and activities. Each activity blends into others, each affecting the performance of others. In a clinical supervisor's daily activites, these functions may be viewed as a vicious cycle without beginning or end. However, if one thinks of the managerial process as a cycle consisting of five functions, it greatly simplifies one's job

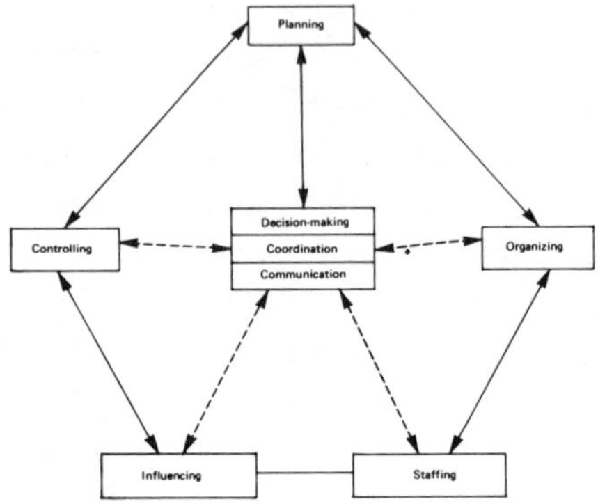

Fig. 10. Management flow chart

of supervising. By organizing these tasks into functions, or clusters, the demands of the job of supervisor become systematic and achievable (see Figure 10).

To summarize, the clinical supervisor performs three basic functions: managerial, educational, and supportive, each of which focuses on the various programmatic needs: those of the agency, the client, and the counselor. The synthesis of these roles is crucial.

How Do Clinical Supervision, Case Management, and In-Service Training Differ?

The three roles of the clinical supervisor (educator, supporter, and administrator) are different from the roles involved in administrative supervision. If leadership is the act of coordinating and motivating individuals to achieve desired ends, then clinical leadership is performed by motivating rather than by sanctioning. It takes into account the individual counselor and the client's needs far more than does administrative supervision.

The tasks of the supervisor as administrator and clinician can be broken down into three primary functions: clinical supervision, coordination for case management, and training (in-service and extra-mural). Often in the alcoholism field these three functions are merged in the minds of supervisors, without clear distinctions between the functions. This further contributes to the confusion over what is clinical supervision. Yet, each function differs significantly in its goals, purposes, methodologies, programmatic focus, and structure.

Table 3 shows the differences between clinical supervision, case management, and training. Case management may take place among staff members of a unit and/or among the total treatment program. The goal of case management is ultimately administrative in focus, involving the gathering, sharing, and reviewing of information and data concerning all aspects of the program's functioning. It may address the concerns of clients, but this is not the primary focus of the activity, and it is incidental to the administrative/management functions associated with the coordination of client flow and the continuity of care.

Case management seeks to guarantee appropriate planning and treatment assignments. The methods employed are briefer case reviews, group discussion, and presentations by the management staff.

Staff training refers to all of the activities of an agency which might enhance the job-related knowledge, skills, and attitudes of its total personnel. It includes lectures, workshops, institutes, conferences, informational networks, discussion groups, experiential sessions, etc.

The goal of staff training is to further develop the knowlege and skills of the counselors to ensure the highest quality of service. It is an educational process which is often cognitive and didactic in nature. It is generally conducted within units, but may be inter-unit and interdisciplinary in nature.

The focus of training is primarily topical, academic, and theoretical, and involves methods such as role playing, psychodrama, small group discussion, lectures, audiovisual presentations, field observations, other experiential techniques, etc.

The concept of training can also be expanded to include

Table 3. Differences in Case Management, Training, and Clinical Supervision

	Case management	*Training*	*Clinical supervision*
Goal	Information gathering and sharing	Knowledge and skill orientation	Clinical skill development
	Program administration	Informational and educational	
Structure	By unit or full staff	By unit or full staff	One-to-one and/or small groups (2 to 4 persons)
	Interdisciplinary	Interdisciplinary	Generally intradisciplinary
Focus	Coordination of client flow	Topical	Practical counselor/client needs: transference, counter-transferences, catharsis, abreaction, inter- intrapersonal interactions, treatment planning and execution
	Case planning, continuity of care	Academic	
		Theoretical	
Methods	Group discussion	Lecture, teaching	Intensive, in-depth case presentations and discussion
	Briefer case review	Role playing	Use of audio and videotapes
		Use of audio-visuals	Role plays and experiential techniques
		Experiential sessions	

extramural training provided by an agency for other professionals, or for entry-level students seeking to gain initial exposure to counseling. This would encompass activities such as field placements, internships, postdoctoral placements, field observations, and conferences conducted by the agency for community and civic groups.

Finally, the primary goal of clinical supervision is the skill development of staff, teaching counselors what they need to know to be able to provide specific services to specific clients. It focuses on the practical issues of the client–counselor relationship, how to facilitate change in treatment, group dynamics and interactions, how to deal with transference and countertransference issues, inter- and intrapersonal problems, abreaction, treatment planning and execution, etc.

The methods employed in supervision are intensive case review and analysis, utilizing "live materials" such as audiovisual presentations, direct or indirect observation of counseling situations, verbatims, etc. Counselors are often requested to present in-depth case analysis, including significant interactions, treatment goals, objectives, and outcomes, etc. Clinical supervision is typically performed on a one-to-one or small group basis (two to four members per group). This allows for peer interaction between counselors and a group learning milieu.

The differences between the three activities, case management, training, and clinical supervision, must be clearly understood as distinct ingredients for successful programming. The three interface yet are also clearly different.

Chapter 4

MODELS OF CLINICAL SUPERVISION

Lest a person think of himself as a "model" clinical supervisor, he should remember that Webster's Dictionary defines a model as a small copy or imitation of an original. In the context of this book, a model is viewed as a guide, a plan for the delivery of clinical supervision, a pattern for training that determines the form, method, and style of supervision.

This chapter presents a number of different styles of supervision, the Basic and Advanced (Bicycle) Problem-solving Model, the Interpersonal Process Recall Model, the Tucker Cocounselor Sequential Model, Mueller and Kell Conflict Model, Caplan Consultation Model, and the Truax and Carkhuff Didactic/Experiential Model.

The sine quae non of these models are two absolutes that determine the focus of supervision: (1) What a teacher presents is less important than how he teaches it. (2) The supervisor's perception and use of power is the key to the clinical supervisory process. Discrepant theoretical orientations between the supervisor and the counselor impact upon the quality of supervision and the use of power.

The relationship of the supervisor and the counselor is the major factor in determining the counselor's perception of the quality of the supervisory experience. Technical aspects of supervision do not appear to be the primary determinants of the counselors' response to training. The supervisor–trainee relationship is a social reality, an actual interactional situation subject to the general interpersonal processes of human intercourse.

The key to this interpersonal process is how the clinical supervisor utilizes the authority vested in her position. This depends on the social agreements around the right of and limitations on the use of power. Ekstein and Wallerstein (1972) warn of the misuse of authority to satisfy inappropriate supervisory wishes for students to identify with him, such as disciple collecting.

Szasz (1961) postulates an inverse relationship between authority and the effectiveness of supervision. If a supervisor is too powerful, she will be viewed as an indoctrinator, and counselors will feel the need to comply with the wishes and teachings of the supervisor. When power is renunciated, there is a facilitation of a positive learning relationship.

Although this cannot always be done, especially since counselors and supervisors are not equals, there is a need to establish an asymmetrical collaborative power relationship between the two parties. As a supervisor utilizes the force of his personality to establish authority, the relationship between both parties grows and learning is enhanced.

Authority is the "legitimate power to initiate work, to command and allocate resources, delegated from above and affirmed from below." Substance abuse agencies, however, are characterized by what might be termed the "pudding" concept of authority. The roles of supervisors and staff are merged so that power and authority become confused and uncertain. Authority is marginally endowed in the *position* of the supervisor, but rarely in the *person* of the supervisor. Power becomes amorphous and uncertain in these social service agencies.

A basic source of conflict for supervisors arises over the confusion between responsibility and authority. Supervisors are endowed with the former, but rarely with the latter. They must be given the authority to act, to issue directives and commands, to exercise decision making, to demand obedience when necessary, and have the power to back up these actions. Supervisors derive this power from top management.

Power can take various forms: reinforcement, position, referent, and expert. Reinforcement power is derived from the supervisor's ability to give raises, provide promotions, office space, favorable work responsibilities and assignments, scheduling, training and travel opportunities, positive references, approval and commendation, etc. It also involves the ability to exert negative reinforcements, such as disciplinary action, poor job performance ratings, degrading work assignments, rejections, etc. Positive reinforcements, obviously, are more powerful and effective in the long run in motivating staff to perform and improve. The merit system of civil service works against reinforcement power as an effective mechanism for eliciting behaviors for it routinizes performance. To get promoted in state or municipal service often involves "keeping one's nose clean." Also, in most public agencies there is little flexibility and potential for rewards since they operate on minimal budgets with few career ladder possibilities. Many counselor jobs are dead-end positions.

The same can be said for the use of negative reinforcement measures as means of providing power to the supervisor. Most civil service positions in public health agencies are permanent, with few steps to be taken to discipline staff. It reinforces the saying, "Civil service workers are like Nike missiles: they don't work and you can't fire them."

When a clinical supervisor utilizes reinforcement power as a means of eliciting a response from counselors, it is generally perceived as coercive. The supervisor is criticized as displaying a personally antagonistic style, as being challenging, competitive, and exploiting the one-up position. They are viewed as being disparaging to students, downgrading them, and pushing their own value system. Counselors often comment: "He is always critical of me." "She always gives advice and is interested in impressing me with her knowledge, control, and decision-making rights." "I feel like a puppet counselor."

Although not all clinical supervisors who utilize reinforcement power are coercive and controlling in their style, counselors under them generally perceive them this way.

Positional power means that the supervisor, by the nature of the title, is worthy of power and authority. In substance abuse agencies, legitimate positional power may be blurred if the staff does not feel that the individual in the supervisory role warrants that position. This is especially true in the light of the polarization between professional and paraprofessional counselors, degreed and nondegreed, and recovered alcoholic and staff members who are not alcoholics. "Just because you are the supervisor does not mean that I have to respect you." "I was doing Twelve-Step work before you were still wet behind the ears." Thus, position in social service agencies does not necessarily grant one authority and power.

Referent power is derived from the employees' need to be liked and thought of as competent. This can best occur when there is a positive relationship between the supervisor and staff. "I want to be liked by my supervisor" is the message. The supervisor is seen as a professional to be emulated or as a role model to follow. Approval and commendation by the supervisor is sought. These supervisors typically are viewed by their counselors as being scholarly, cultured, experienced, businesslike, and anxiety-arousing because of their intellectual prestige. There is a sense of parochialism conveyed. Students comment: "His remarks are like lecturettes." "I feel like a pupil, in a one-way knowledge relationship." "I am unable to get close to him." "She always seems detached from me."

The most effective type of power is expert power, based on

the special knowledge, skill, and competency of the supervisor. He has something valuable and desirable to give to the staff. One's credibility as a professional is central to expert power. In the substance abuse field, degrees are not sufficient to endow one with expert power. Alcoholism counselors are often characterized by an antiintellectualism and antiacademia that mitigates against degrees as prerequisites for expert power. One's competencies are more important than the "chicken-scratchings" after one's name. To gain expert power, one must display his abilities as a counselor.

If a supervisor sees himself as clinically incompetent, he should reexamine his position and question whether or not he is inappropriately assigned. He will not be able to win the respect of staff and gain expert power.

To be effective in utilizing power, the authority of the clinical supervisor should be seen as collaborative. Supervisors should display a personally engaging style characterized by:

- warmth, sensitivity, "likeableness," egalitarianism
- a good sense of humor
- open-mindedness, not bound by tradition
- intuitive in approach
- willing to take risks in therapy
- inspiring
- using the force of personality and competencies rather than position to gain authority

Counselors studying under such a supervisor comment: "My supervisor is open, enabling people to be open with him." "She relates to people easily." "I feel comfortable with her, like I can disclose things to her." "She is charismatic and nondefensive." "She is interested in my career development."

The key to these four styles of power is not found solely in the intrapsychic dynamics of the supervisor but also in the eye of the beholder. For supervisors exercising collaborative, expert power in dyadic relationships, they must work with counselors who are not overawed by authority and position, who are willing to assume an active initiating role, and be able to collaborate.

Reinforcement power is often misperceived by those who feel resentful over the power and status invested in the supervisor. Referent power may be sought out by supervisees looking for a powerful, professional guru. Persons impressed by institutional status and prestige may need to have an omnipotent clinical supervisor.

In sum, the interaction of supervisor and supervisee determines the supervisor's exercise of authority and power and the supervisee's perception of that power utilization.

In many substance abuse agencies, conflicts arise in supervision over the confusion of the "pudding" concept of authority. Authority and power become vague terms where staff individualism and autonomy are cornerstones of the field. Where there are few psychotherapeutic paradigms, it is difficult to endow power in a clinical supervisor simply on the basis of position or reinforcements. He must earn that power by his own clinical competency, as demonstrated in direct observation of the supervisor in action. Resistance is best overcome by earning the right to exert power.

The supervisor can aid his cause by doing the following:

Clarify lines of authority via an agency organizational chart

Develop job descriptions for all positions, including his own

Ensure that his superiors will support him when action is necessary

Develop his own expert power by displaying his clinical skills and competency

The second absolute for clinical supervisory models is the concept of cognitive consistency: areas of congruence or similarity between the supervisor and supervisee and the effect on interpersonal attraction determines the "success" of the supervision in the eyes of the counselor. Discrepant theoretical orientations negatively impact on the student's perceptions of the supervisor. As supervisor and counselor share common ideas, the interpersonal attraction between the two increases.

Similarly if a counselor perceives a basic discrepancy about his skills, he will be less likely to share information, discuss goals and objectives, etc. with the clinical supervisor. Issues that play a part in the feeling of congruence are counseling philosophy and treatment approaches; professional affiliation; prior professional experiences; personal experiences with alcohol, drugs, or other life problems; sex of both parties; the supervisor's perception of the supervisee; and the proximity of the work setting. In sum, these absolutes are perceived by staff as determining the initial nature of the supervisory relationship. All models of clinical supervision must take these two issues into account in developing a plan for supervision.

Models of Supervision

Several different models of supervision have been developed. The Kadushin Role Model for clinical supervision is the basic model for this book. This is a combination of two approaches: the first is an existential, trainee-oriented approach that views the supervisor as dealing with the counselor's personal and professional growth, self-awareness, and understanding. The attitudes, feelings, and emotions of the supervisee are key to the process. He has the major responsibility for what he wants to learn, his job needs, and his relationship to the client. This book also utilizes the Kadushin approach that is didactic, task-oriented, viewing the supervisor as concerned with the clinical skills of the counselor, his thinking, and training needs. The supervisor is responsible for what is taught, focusing on what the counselor is doing with patients.

The combination of these two approaches forms the basic model for this text. The following pages will present other models for supervision. Most of the models have one process in common: the problem-solving process. This process for clinical supervision will be discussed first.

Basic and Advanced (Bicycle) Problem-solving Method

The basic problem-solving mode of the scientific method can be applied to the clinical supervisory process (Fig. 11). The first step in the method is the recognition of a difficulty, such as a particular patient problem and/or clinical impasse. It may be an obstacle which the counselor does not know how to surmount. It may be a gap between where she is and where she would like to be in her clinical functioning. In the clinical supervisory process it involves the identification and recognition of the clinical problems of the counselor.

The second step in the method is an analysis of the difficulty that results in a provisional understanding of its nature and characteristics and probable ways of dealing with the diffi-

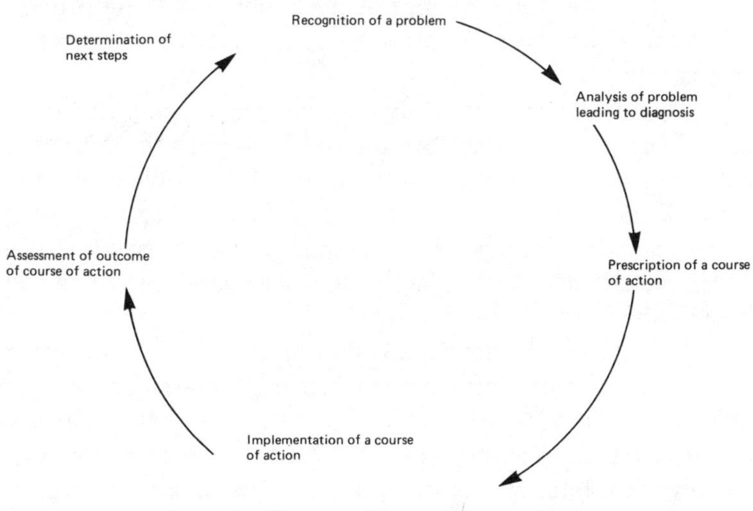

Fig. 11. Basic problem-solving method.

culty in a successful manner. In counseling, this is the diagnostic process. In clinical supervision, this is an analysis process undertaken by the supervisor and supervisee.

The third step is to consider all available alternatives, to select a course of treatment, and to plan and organize an attack on the problem. In clinical terms, this is the prescription and treatment planning process. In clinical supervisory terms, this is the goal setting of the problem-solving process done by the counselor with the aid of the supervisor.

The next step is the implementation of the course of action, or the testing out of a particular clinical approach to resolve the counseling impasse or difficulty. The fifth step is an assessment of the outcome of the course of action, and finally, the assimilation of the learned behavior into a systematic and coherent approach to treatment.

A more sophisticated approach to the basic problem-solving method might be termed the Bicycle (bi-cycle) approach (Fig. 12). In comparing this approach with the basic method, in the former steps 1 through 8 in the outer cycle of health care operations are preparatory to the problem-solving steps. Steps 9 through 12 are the sequence of the problem-solving process. This method has been adapted to the clinical supervisory process as follows.

Step 1 involves the setting of priorities of counselor training and supervisory needs. Steps 2 and 3 establish the data bases and the organization of the data for use. The problem-oriented record-keeping system is an example of the adaption of this step to the treatment process. The discrepancy analysis needs assessment procedures described in this text are adaptions of this step to the clinical supervisory process.

Miller (1967) writes regarding this step that "adult learning is not most efficiently achieved through systematic subject instruction; it is accomplished by involving learners in identifying problems and seeking ways to solve them. It does not come in categorical bundles but in a growing need to know" (Miller, 1967, p. 320).

For this reason, Fleisher (1974) begins the clinical supervi-

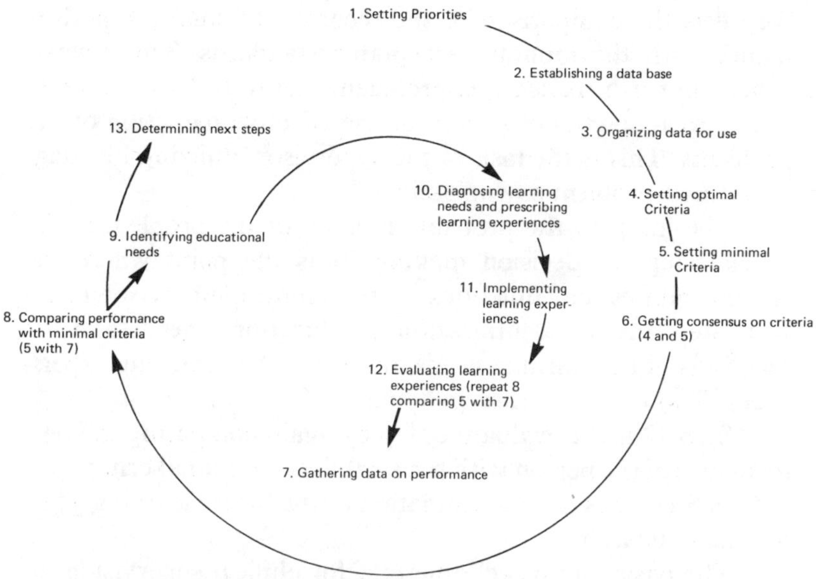

Fig. 12. The Bicycle process. From Charters, Alexander N. & Blakely, R. J. Management of continuing learning. In *Fostering the growing need to learn.* Rockville, Md.: Dept. of Health, Education, and Welfare, 1973. p 6.

sory process at steps 4 and 5—setting of optimal and minimal criteria for standards of performance of interest to the supervisees. "Usually people want to learn how to derive and handle data before they are willing to invest time and effort setting priorities" (Fleisher, 1974, p. 202).

Steps 4 through 6 involve the process of auditing the educational components in the clinical supervisory process. The greatest impact in the process is exerted in the step where the counselors themselves decide what the standards of performance should be. This is the key step in the discrepancy analysis process.

Step 7 is the data gathering of actual performance, or the review of the "live material" by the counselor and supervisor.

Step 8 is the comparison of the records of actual job performance with the minimal acceptable standards. This reveals deficits in performance, i.e., proficiency gaps. It does not, however, reveal courses of action for the effective reduction of the problems. This is the task of the supervisor, utilizing his diagnostic and problem-soving skills.

The jump to the probable remedy of the problem is the crucial step for decision making. It is the point where the responsibilities and functions of the clinical supervisor intersect. Step 9 is the identification of educational needs and the diagnosis of the learning needs and prescribed learning experiences. The remedy is herein sought.

Step 12 is the evaluative step by again comparing the performance of the person with the established minimal criteria for action. Step 13 is the determination of the future learning goals for the counselor.

The basic and bicycle method for clinical supervision involve a simple process for determining the actions of the supervisor. It is not a method that deals with interactional patterns and issues, but is a scientific, methodological way of viewing clinical supervision. It can be seen as the foundation for the subsequent models to be discussed in this chapter.

Interpersonal Process Recall Model

The Interpersonal Process Recall (IPR) Model for clinical supervision provides a method for analyzing in supervision the interactional system between a speaker (S) and a listener (L). The speaker (client) presents a personal problem and the listener (counselor) uses the skills she has learned to respond empathically and therapeutically. The IPR model for clinical supervision involves a careful examination by the supervisor/-supervisee of this interaction.

"I" in IPR indicates that the interaction is between persons; "P" indicates that there is a flow and interchange (both covert and overt) which occurs requiring a particular response from the listener. In clinical supervision, the focus is upon the response (or the recall) and involves the following steps:

1. Clarification of the role of the recaller in IPR. The recaller (the clinical supervisor) is viewed as a facilitative inquirer who helps listeners and speakers to examine and learn from their interaction, demonstrating the appropriate use of open-ended questioning as a therapeutic and learning technique.
2. Focus on the listener's response in the IPR.
3. During recall the listener (counselor) explores her feelings and responses and receives feedback on what was done and areas needing improvement.
4. Clarification of the role of the speaker (client). The recaller (clinical supervisor) focuses on the feelings of the client that may have been missed in the interaction. The listener receives feedback on these feelings and his response to them.
5. Clarification of the role of the listener (counselor) in IPR, which is to listen and respond to speaker feelings and concerns, helping to clarify conflicts, owning feelings when appropriate, exploring his own feelings and responses during recall, and receiving feedback after recall.
6. During IPR the other supervisees watch for nonverbal behavior, formulate feedback, watch the recaller, discuss the interactional process, etc.

"Live material" is the textbook for the IPR model for clinical supervision. The supervisor must set up the interactions to be reviewed by carefully selecting relevant and potent material. The concern or topic of the interaction chosen should be personally relevant to the listener (counselor). The focus of the recall should remain on the listener to allow for self-exploration of the listener role. At the beginning of the recall, the recaller questions should be directed to "L" only. As the recall progresses, "R" should continue to direct questions to "L" but she may choose to draw in the other counselors as a resource to "L's" discoveries.

The "R" in the IPR model is more directive than in most other models, questioning, probing, facilitating discussion, and modeling behavior when appropriate. The supervisor may choose to participate in the speaker role as a role-playing method. By so doing, she would present the real concerns of the speaker. If cosupervision is possible, one can act as a speaker while the second acts as a recaller. It is recommended, however, in the IPR model that other group members be utilized in the speaker role.

The supervisor develops an appropriate line of open-ended questions dealing with the interactional process. The listener is taught not to ask "yes-no," "true-false," multiple choice, value-laden, or judgmental questions with built-in answers. The clinical supervisor models this behavior by asking: "What was going on here?" and not "Why did you say this?" "How did it develop?" and not "This is what should have developed."

The following is a list of sample open-ended recaller questions:

What do you think the speaker was thinking at that point?

What do you think the speaker was feeling?

What were you—the listener—thinking? Feeling?

How do you feel about your response at that point?

How do you hear the speaker reacting to your response?

What other ways could you have responded?

What got in the way of your saying that?

Were you having thoughts or feelings which got in the way of your listening to the speaker? (Roadblocks) What were they?

How were you perceiving the speaker then?

How did you want the speaker to perceive you?

Counselor frustration generally comes from the implicit demand that she discipline and train herself to be more attentive to her clients, herself, and the relationship. The paradox between statements and questions is resolved when the counselor learns how to make reflective statements and ask exploratory questions (as in problem-solving process). She may take either kind of response, depending on the appropriateness of their impact.

During the recall the supervisor asks the rest of the group to remain silent. Their task during recall is to listen to the interaction and the recall process and then offer feedback to the listener. The supervisor's task during the discussion is to help the trainees interpret what has happened in the interaction and in the recall, and to make certain that the listener receives clear feedback about her counseling strengths and weaknesses during the interaction.

In the IPR there are a number of do's and don'ts for the supervisor. The don'ts are those responses/actions that do not facilitate communication; whereas the do's will facilitate. It is a checklist of behaviors that might properly be applied to most clinical supervisory models.

DON'T	*DO*
• Have answers in mind rather than lead counselors to their own point of view.	• Encourage self-discovery by conveying attitudes that the client/counselor are capable of finding their own answers.
• Seem disinterested or distracted.	• Show involvement by facilitative gestures (smiling, eye contact, head nodding, etc.)
• Ask loaded questions.	• Ask open-ended questions.
• Be critical, punishing, or judgmental of counselors.	• Be positive, supportive, and nonjudgmental.

• Appear impatient, not waiting for the counselor's own discoveries.	• Be patient and willing to wait for the counselor to arrive at his own conclusions.
• Be too wordy, monopolizing conversation.	• Keep focus on the counselor.
• Generalize instead of focusing on the here and now specifics (the interaction, the recall).	• Attend to counselor affect and behavior at the time of the interaction and during recall.
• Interject one's own interpretation of events and affect.	• Ask counselor's interpretation of events and affect.
• Be anxious and unsure of oneself.	• Be assertive and in control.
• Encourage counselors to make "textbook" responses.	• Allow counselors to learn the impact of concepts on the speaker/listener and the appropriateness of responses in specific interactions.

Tucker Cocounselor Sequential Model

Tucker (1976) presents a cocounselor sequential model for clinical supervision based on the premise of observable, definite, and systematic phases over the course of the training. The model was developed through work with graduate students in counseling psychology paired in cotherapist teams conducting primarily family therapy.

In this model, the goals of clinical supervision are:

to have the counselors deal with their attitudes, feelings, and reactions to each other;
to review and critique dynamics in therapy;
to generalize about the process in the clinical situation;

to establish future goals and objectives for clinical sessions; and,

to verbalize responses about the clinical supervisor.

The goals should be attempted in a systematic fashion. The first step in the model is to have the counselors deal with their reactions to each other and to the clinical situation. This is done in the presence of a clinical supervisory group. Initially, the tendency is to minimize the distortion and bias of the reactions. The supervisor plays a teacher/questioner/facilitator role to enhance exchange and dialogue.

The issues to be discussed at this place in the sequence are:

cooperation and competition;

initiation and support;

the appropriate utilization of confrontation, self-disclosure, and analysis;

passive vs. dominance roles; and,

general feelings and attitudes to fellow counselors.

Tucker provides the following examples of the issues in this sequence:

> Richard and Charles were meeting with a mother and her teenage child: The counselor says to the mother, "When James leaves, how will that be for you?" The second counselor follows that question by asking, "How will it feel to be alone?"
>
> In this case, the mother begins to speak about her son, avoiding the questions asked. In the group clinical supervisory session later the two counselors shared the feeling that they were interfering with each other in the process. "It was my intervention and you should have stayed out of it. I am angry at you for interfering."
>
> The second counselor responds that he was not really thinking about it. "I just felt that you were so on target that I repeated what you said." The clinical supervisor intervened, "So Richard, you allowed your angry feelings to get in your way, and did not pursue with the family what might have been a fruitful area of exploration?"

> Charles states, "I don't think you trust me, Richard."
>
> Richard states, "It's just that I got so hooked into my anger."
>
> Supervisor, "What happens when you feel angry like that?"
>
> Richard, "I feel helpless and don't know what to do ."
>
> Supervisor, "You could put your hand out and gently block Charles and say, 'Wait a minute, I would like to pursue this further.'" (Tucker, 1976, p. 4).

As illustrated here, in this phase of clinical supervision the task of the leader is to focus on the feelings of the counselors, and interpersonal issues, such as rapport, honesty, trust, etc.

Counselors are generally, at this point, reticent to deal with inter- and intrapersonal issues or to disagree on theoretical and/or therapeutic issues in the presence of each other. Disagreement is not legitimized by the group. Competitiveness among counselors is present although not on the surface and not always verbalized.

The second goal of the sequential model is to deal in the supervisory sessions with an analysis of clinical interactions. The order or sequence of the supervisory process is reversed in this model as compared to other models: usually the analysis of the observable interactions are dealt with prior to the inter- and intrapersonal concerns due to a perceived resistance by most to the latter. In the sequential model, the dynamics of the counseling session are analyzed via a diagnostic/evaluative process. The following perceptions are requested:

Identification of the interactional patterns and processes
Interpersonal functioning of the client
Intrapsychic functionality/disfunctionality
Communication styles (verbal and nonverbal)
Developmental history
Actual observed behaviors of clients

The purpose of this sequence is to heighten the identification and analysis skills of the counselors and to avoid theoretical, hypothetical postulating.

The third sequence is for the counselors to generalize from the specific behaviors and functioning observed to overall issues, such as client resistance, counselor's use of self, ethics, and professionalism in counseling, treatment planning and goal setting, psychotherapeutic modalities, psychopathology, and client motivation. The clinical supervisor assumes an active teacher role providing generalized theoretical, conceptual information to the counselors, sharing experiences and facilitating group discussion. The current state of the art of therapy is provided at this phase.

Fourth, the sessions address future treatment planning and the development of the counselors' individualized therapy style. In the earlier sequences, supervisees tend to deaccentuate differences, conflict, and disagreements. By this phase, individuality is encouraged and enhanced by the supervisor's actions. It is a time for creative growth with equal participation of all group members and less defensive reactions. There is an evaluation and synthesis of new ideas, suggestion, and an exploration of alternative approaches to counseling. There is risk-taking, hypothesizing, and "I would" statements made, along with "you should" comments.

A variety of techniques and approaches are given by the clinical supervisor. Issues addressed are specific interventions and responses, roles of therapists, potential treatment outcomes and goal setting, strategies for implementation, and viable alternative counselor behaviors. Supervisees are at this point able to react to suggestions from other staff members so that they can develop and evolve their own therapeutic styles. Theoretical orientations and individual personalities begin to develop and appear now.

The last step in this model is to deal with the response of the counselors to the clinical supervisor. These sessions resemble sensitivity training groups where there is open discussion of the supervisor, group dynamics and processes, individual group members and behaviors, closure and termination issues, group change, and unfinished group tasks. To facilitate this step it is useful to utilize "live material" from the supervisory sessions, such as videotapes of previous sessions. Issues such as dealing with substandard performance by counselors, expressed hostility and anger in the group, sharing and intimacy, the group's emotional tone, personal problems, sexual issues in the group, and sensitive and unresolved problems, are all covered.

This model is another way of analyzing the clinical supervisory process, and although there are components common to all of the models, this is another view of that process.

Mueller and Kell Conflict Model

Mueller and Kell (1972), in their book *Coping with Conflict: Supervising Counselors and Psychotherapists,* present a clinical supervisory model similar to the psychotherapeutic process based on a conflict resolution model for change. It is stated that all human relationships are characterized by anxiety and conflict, fears, hopes, expectations, vulnerabliities, sensitivities, uncertainties, and inadequacies. Clinical supervision is a series of in-depth analyses of personality and the conflicts generated through clinical interactions. It uses an inductive casework approach.

However, clinical supervision differs from other interpersonal relationships because the primary focus ought to be on anxiety, stress, and human conflicts within the client, the counselor, and the clinical supervisor. According to Mueller, conflict is the source of material for discussion in supervision. It is the curriculum, the syllabus for the course of study. The three sources of conflict addressed in clinical supervision are the client in relation to himself and others, the counselor and client in relation to each other, and the counselor and the clinical supervisior in relation to each other.

The manner in which these conflicts arise and are resolved defines the clinical supervisory process. Mueller points out that counselor conflict is generally not with problems in his grasp of theoretical knowledge or psychotherapeutic theories but with the interactions between the involved parties: client, counselor himself, and the clinical supervisor.

The goal of clinical supervision in this model is to teach the therapist to be therapeutic. This inevitably converges on therapy for the therapist, which is acceptable in this model. The foundation for the clinical supervisory process and relationships involves examining with equal intensity the client's and counselor's feelings, fantasies, anxieties, etc.; and examining the sequence of events involved in the conflict, the how and why of the stress, the counselor's reaction to the conflict, etc.

In teaching the therapist to be therapeutic, the supervisor must address the conflicts between himself and the counselor. This involves an exploration of the following issues:

Trust vs. mistrust conflicts (with reciprocal trust being a necessary prelude to collaboration)

Security vs. trustworthiness

Creativity vs. constraints

Initiative vs. integration

Emotional dependence vs. growth

The supervisory process, as in psychotherapy, usually reaches an impasse. Mueller defines this as a disagreement between the counselor and the clinical supervisor, or between the client and the counselor. The key in supervision is that the impasse stage be anticipated, encountered, and resolved by the supervisor by the following methods:

Differentiating the source of the stress behind the impasse.

Awareness of the dynamics of the impasse which may involve an ambivalence in the client, counselor, or supervisor.

Reconstruction of the relationship by expanding the conflicted feelings experienced by the counselor/client, and

> accurately experiencing these feelings into the clinical supervisory relationship, without stimulating regression. The supervisor helps by releasing the feelings, by identifying and freeing the therapeutic deadlock, by a comparison between what is felt and what is "real." The supervisor slowly expands feelings and confronts the actual "precipitating events for their occurrence."

Mueller views the process of differentiation as a necessary prelude to growth for the counselor. This is because novice counselors feel the need to help the client, and to be adequate in that helping process. This leads to a confusion over therapeutic actions and nurturance, which tends to be an overprotectiveness and "mothering" process.

According to the conflict model, the clinical supervisory process goes through a series of stages, each with its own learning needs and goals. The "developing phase" is characterized by efforts by trainees to learn about themselves and each other, to establish trust, reconciling expectations and differences of opinion. The focus is primarily upon intra- and intersupervisee conflicts. The goal of this stage of supervision is the establishment of a desired maturity.

The "mature phase," according to Mueller, focuses on the collaborative work of conflict resolution related to clients, the counselor, and the clinical supervisor. The goal is to release the potential of the counselor for future growth, freeing interactions, fantasies, and feelings. The clinical supervisory relationship is characterized by a greater spontaneity with energies tested and expanded. The clinical supervisor addresses means of resolving interpersonal conflicts between the counselor and the supervisor in a less regressive manner.

The "terminating phase" occurs when a deepening of learning has occurred, and the trainee is able to resolve his own conflicts without the clinical supervisor's assistance. The stage lays the groundwork for long-term growth by the counselor so that he can be able to help himself help clients.

In comparison with other clinical supervisory models, the Mueller Conflict Model is fairly consistent in principle and strategies. The major difference in this model is the extreme emphasis upon the conflict resolution aspects of the clinical supervisory process vs. the skill development and competency issues.

In summary, these various techniques characterize the Mueller and Kell Conflict Model for clinical supervision. The overall theme for the supervisory relationship is the identification and resolution of interactional conflicts.

Caplan Consultation Model

As Monty Python's Flying Circus began its television series with the words "and now for something completely different," so we begin a discussion of the consultation model for clinical supervision. Gerald Caplan (1970), in *The Theory of Mental Health Consultation,* presents a different approach to clinical supervision which he identifies as more of a consultative than a supervisory/educational process.

Caplan differentiates between supervision and consultation: Supervision is viewed as primarily focusing on administrative and clinical responsibilities. It is, according to Caplan, an ongoing process of inspecting the work of supervisees by a person who is high on the hierarchical power structure. Consultation, on the other hand, is an ad hoc process, an interaction or short series of interactions, arising out of current work-related problems. It is not regular in its scheduling and is conducted in a nonpower latent situation. The only "power" issues in consultation involve the authority of one's ideas. (Although Caplan defines the learning process that takes place between supervisor and counselor as consultation, this definition is closer to the staff development and in-service training definition used in this book.)

Clinical supervision in this model (or consultation as Caplan defines it) has no direct responsibility for implementing remedial action but only offers helpful clarifications, diagnostic formulations, and advice to the counselor. The latter, though, is free to accept or reject this advice. Additionally, the consultation process focuses on adding knowledge and insight to the counselor on areas of confusion, ignorance, or misunderstanding. Caplan outlines four types of consultation:

Client-centered case consultation

Consultee-centered case consultation

Program-centered administrative consultation

Consultee-centered administrative consultation

(This book's definition of clinical supervision comes closest to the second type of consultation—consultee-centered case consultation—which Caplan states occurs in consultee-centered consultation seminars, specialized practitioner workshops, and specialized supervisory experiences, such as field internships or fellowship training experiences.)

The focus of the consultee-centered case consultation is on a lack of knowledge, lack of skills, lack of self-confidence, or lack of professional objectivity. The following consultee issues may be addressed, according to Caplan: identification, transference, characterological distortions of perception and behavior, and, theme inferences, which Caplan defines as an unresolved problem, an experienced defeat, a frustrated need, or a negative emotional tone of rankling failure.

The key ingredients to the training provided in the consultation model are as follows:

Building a consultant/consultee relationship by obtaining and establishing proximity and a contract between parties, maintaining sanctions, etc.

Building channels of communication

Overseeing communication obstacles, such as distortions of perception and expectation or conflicts of interest, etc.

Arousing a sense of trust and respect

Developing a common verbal and nonverbal language, and,

Establishing ground rules for collaboration.

These steps involve dealing with anxieties, fostering a mutual respect, maintaining confidentiality, and providing a therapeutic role model for the consultee.

Throughout this process, the consultant/consultee relationship should never focus on psychotherapeutic issues within the counselor himself. Consultation is not therapy, and does not deal with intrapsychic or interactional issues except as they directly relate to clinical issues.

The Caplan "clinical supervisory" model differs significantly from other models in its definition, focus, methodology, scheduling, and intensity.

Truax and Carkhuff Didactic/Experiential Model

Truax (1967) defines clinical supervision as a therapeutic process involving the shaping of the counselor's personality and behavior and focusing on his personal growth and development. The learning that occurs in clinical supervision, according to Truax, occurs within the context of an interpersonal relationship free of threat and which facilitates self-exploration. It involves the combining of didactic and experiential approaches to training.

The didactic approach involves the shaping of the counselor's professional behavior through the use of basic learning principles. The clinical supervisor, in his role, becomes a teacher/educator who overtly reinforces the counselor's performance of desirable responses and extinquishes those that are undesirable. However, Truax also sees clinical supervision as an expansion and elaboration of the counselor's basic skills, adding knowledge and information as appropriate, but supplied primarily in response to a felt need. The store of knowledge of the supervisor is passed downward in an additive function to an "accepting" student.

This approach is often viewed as fostering a doctrinaire, "technicianship" model. However, Truax states that when combined with an experiential approach it becomes a vibrant approach to learning.

The experiential approach involves a nurturing of feelings, developing a sense of freedom, safety, openness, and a willingness to take risks. There is an instituting of certain attitudinal conditions, in an upward flow from the trainee's experiences to the clinical supervisor, in an inductive manner. Carl Rogers' client-centered approach to therapy (1951) is the best illustration of this model of clinical supervision.

> The student should develop his own orientation to psychotherapy out of his own experience. In my estimation every effective therapist has built his own orientation to therapy within himself and out of his own experience with his clients or patients. It is quite true that this orientation as finally developed may be such that it closely resembles that of others, or closely resembles the orientation to which he was exposed. Nevertheless, the responses made by the effective therapist in his interviews are not made in a certain way because that is the psychoanalytic way, or the client-centered way, or the Adlerian way, they are made because the therapist has found that type of response effective in his own experience. Thus the aim of a training program in therapy should be to turn out individuals who have an independent and open attitude toward their own experience in working with clients. If this is achieved, then they can continually formulate and reformulate and revise their own approach to the individuals with whom they are working in such a way that their approach results in a more constructive and effective help. (Rogers, 1951, p. 438).

Truax combines these two approaches into an integrated, systematic model for clinical supervision. This is a see-saw, interactional process of inductive generalizations from clinical experience qualifying the deductions of earlier experience.

The knowledge of the clinical supervisor is brought into the session in a therapeutic supervisor/supervisee relationship. It becomes a special form of psychotherapy.

This self-exploration process is directly related to personality growth and change, which is, according to Truax, a primary goal of clinical supervision. It involves an operationalizing of learning into an integrated system of therapy (self-congruence, nonpossessive warmth, transparency, emphathic understanding, etc.).

There are three basic conditions for clinical supervision in this model:

1. The use of theoretical and clinical illustrations to didactically teach empathy, unconditional positive regard, and counselor genuineness.
2. Demonstrations of counseling sessions are presented at three levels of clinical functioning (high, medium, and low) using an established rating scale.
3. The counselor trains in order to rate himself on these scales. The supervisee is taught to distinguish between different levels of empathic listening, non-possessive warmth, and genuineness in the counseling relationship.

The trainee is then taught to display empathic understanding through the use of "live material" and role-playing experimentation, followed by "single interviews" and ongoing psychotherapeutic contracts.

This model differs from others in its utilization of the client-centered approach to content and process, and the psychotherapeutic emphasis in the clinical supervisory process.

Chapter 5

KEY ISSUES IN CLINICAL SUPERVISION

Determining the Needs of Staff

If a clinical supervisor is to tailor training to the specific needs of the staff, it is essential that he have an accurate reading on those needs. To teach everything to everyone denies individual differences.

How does one determine staff needs? Needs assessments are as ubiquitous and necessary as they are inevitable. In one sense, everytime a supervisor nods her head, or says yes or no in response to a counselor, an assessment is provided. However, formal evaluations of the counselor's strengths and weaknesses are necessary if the counselor is to grow. Evaluations provide an opportunity for seeing both how the individual "trees" and the "whole orchard" are growing.

Assessments by the supervisor provide feedback to the counselor on his needs. They serve to relieve anxieties. Counselors have a chance to receive a different perception on their achievements. This can help to both motivate, direct, and integrate skills. Good evaluations act as reinforcers for change and growth. By determining the needs of one's staff via evaluations, it helps to make the learning conscious for it provides benchmarks on where the person is now and how far she has to go.

Evaluations also provide indicators to the program administrators of needed changes in agency management and personnel. It may point to agency failings in hiring policies. Promotions, dismissals, and re-assignments may be indicated in the evaluations.

Lastly, staff evaluations provide clients a check ensuring that the highest quality of care is being provided. A positive evaluation is an endorsement of the proficiency of service. It provides an assessment of the negative consequences of the counseling offered.

However, the clinical supervisor must be aware that such evaluations may create other problems, such as staff resentment; indications of inadequate management procedures, such as hiring, monitoring, and poor program administration; and dissension among staff when they tend to compare their work against others. In spite of these problems, though, clinical evaluations are necessary to the operations of all programs. The only thing more anxiety-provoking than an evaluation is no evaluation.

Figure 13 portrays a model for measuring success based upon client outcome via measurements of goal attainment and indicators of treatment success. In substances abuse counseling, the goal is to assist clients towards a state of mental, physical, psychological, and social homeostasis. For many treatment agencies, sobriety or nondrug use is the initial (and sole) goal of counseling. However, a combination of sobriety and psychological, emotional, social, and physical health is a more desirable goal. The indicators of success and the procedures by which the goal attainment can be measured may be both formal and informal in nature. Sobriety in the alcoholism community can be determined via the AA grapevine.

The attainment of other counseling goals (emotional and

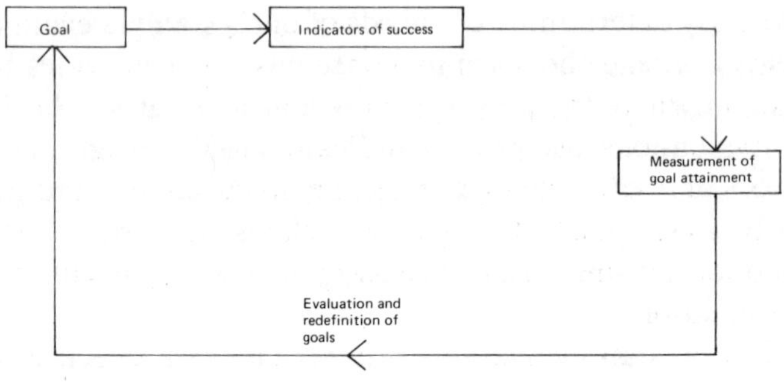

Fig. 13. A model for measuring success.

psychological health) are indicated by job security, financial normalcy, family stability, and freedom from legal problems. These can be measured by way of information derived from other patients, self-reports, and reports from concerned individuals, such as friends, employers, and acquaintances, etc.

As feedback on treatment goal attainment is received by the counselor, a process of evaluation and redefinition is initiated. Client outcome evaluation is difficult to measure and correlate with particular actions of the counselor. The "giant step" from goal attainment to attributing that success to any specific action by the counselor is significant. In sum, client outcome evaluation is not (at least given the present state of the art of evaluation) an acceptable indicator of the counselor's strengths and weaknesses.

Other more acceptable methods for determining the needs of staff are objective measurements of the skills and competencies of counselors, peer and colleague evaluations, and clinical assessments by the supervisor. A combination of these methods is the recommended procedure.

Objective measurements of counselor skills and competencies are beginning to develop and are being field-tested. The Carkhuff/Truax model of helping skills is the most widely utilized and accepted objective measurement of clinical skills. An adaptation of the Carkhuff model for evaluation would be recommended. (For additional information regarding this model, the reader is referred to Valle 1979.)

Evaluations by peers can be provided in small group discussions with staff. Often fellow counselors are more critical than the clinical supervisor. This provides an excellent method for determining the counselors' needs.

In addition to peer evaluations, colleague evaluations are becoming increasingly more important in the field. These are typically conducted by a counselor association and/or credentialling body. These assessments are limited since most are based upon nonclinical issues such as years of employment, length and quality of sobriety, number of contact hours of training, etc. Yet, they can provide some baselines indicating whether or not an individual has the necessary background to probably make her an effective counselor. The obvious drawback of these assessments is that no one really knows the optimal number of years experience and training needed to make an effective counselor. If a person is 18 months sober, will he be a less effective counselor that one 5 years sober?

A bright spot in colleague evaluations is that several credentialling bodies have combined these procedures with objective measurements of knowledge and skill base. Clinical interviews are conducted by the certifying board.

Subjective judgments of the clinical supervisor, however, remain the most accurate statement of the counselors' strengths and weaknesses. These evaluations can be drawn from the following sources:

Counselors' written and verbal records

Audio and/or videotapes of counseling sessions

Direct observation of counseling sessions

Group supervision session performance

Observations of counselor activities at staff meetings, and/or professional conferences

Counselors' correspondence, logs, reports, monthly performance records, etc.

Thus, counselor needs can be identified by clinical supervisors by a discrepancy analysis process examining the two polar positions of "where is the counselor now?" vs. "where should he be?"

The first step in this descrepancy analysis process is to determine the present level of clinical functioning of the staff. Thereupon, the supervisor assesses the desired skills for that counselor, given the job tasks and competencies needed to fulfill these tasks. The difference between these is the skill discrepancy, the various competencies which the counselor needs to further develop.

Several factors must be considered:

1. The data must represent the actual world of the counselor, as it exists now, and as it will be in the future.
2. No needs determination is final; needs statements are tentative.
3. Discrepancies must be identified in terms of skills, competencies, and/or actual behaviors to be achieved.
4. The needs assessment must begin with the mission and tasks of each counselor. For example, an alcoholism counselor may be assessed as needing group counseling skills, when, in fact, his functions never involve clients in groups.

There are a number of guides to assist the clinical supervisor in this assessment process. These guides are contained in the following pages, some of which are to be completed by the supervisor only, others by both supervisor and counselor.

Another form of input regarding counselor skills is a Concept Paper. This provides the supervisor with statements by the counselor on his goals and perceptions of his role as counselor. It further provides a projective assessment of the psychological and emotional functioning of the counselor. The Concept Paper is a 4- to 6-page paper in which counselors describe their approach to clients and answer questions such as:

What is the counselor's philosophical view of people?
What is his view of how people change/grow?
What is his view of psychological health/unhealth?
What are his goals in counseling for clients?
What skills and techniques does he utilize in counseling?
What is his perception of the role of counselor and the client?

Another form of information on counselor needs is a Narrative Statement by the counselor. This provides the clinical supervisor an opportunity to assess the feelings, attitudes, and anxieties of the staff. It is in two parts.

Part I

Part I is a letter addressed to the general public and is recommended to be 750 words in length, answering the following questions: Why are you a counselor? What assets do you possess that aid in being effective? What are the main tasks you perform as a counselor?

Part 2

In Part 2 the counselor is asked to introduce himself, describing his family, friends, etc. and the experiences that led him into counseling. The counselor is asked to describe the background that shaped him into the kind of person he is today. This is an autobiographical statement that serves as a valuable tool to the supervisor and the counselor.

These tests should be completed by the counselor with the supervisor's assistance. Semi-annual testing by the supervisor, at least in the early days of employment, can be a valuable tool in the ongoing needs assessment process.

To identify where the counselor should be, the supervisor must examine the counselor's tasks and the skills needed to perform these tasks. Several competency-based assessments have been conducted by state credentialling associations. The supervisor is well advised to consult with these associations to review the skill analyses.

Discrepancy analysis in not an easy process. It is, though, necessary if the supervisor is to have accurate data on the needs of her counselors, and if the supervisor is to base her actions on more than subjective assessments.

The following assessment forms can be completed by both the supervisor and counselor. Each form can be utilized alone or in combination with other forms in this section, although several forms overlap in their focus and questioning. These forms should be completed at the beginning and throughout the clinical supervisory process. Upon completion of the forms by both supervisor and clinician a processing session should be held wherein both share their impressions and negotiate areas of strength and weakness. This process builds a feeling of risk taking and openness in the relationship, as well as providing the supervisor with necessary data to conduct a discrepancy analysis.

The general principles in assessing counselors are:

Evaluations should be continuous throughout the supervisory sessions, preferably quarterly.

The supervisor and counselor should be aware of the nature and extent of the evaluations to be provided.

Both must agree upon the role that these evaluations will play in performance evaluations and administrative decisions.

Assessments must take into account the realities of the job itself, its nature, the type and range of clients seen, the complexity of the tasks, etc.

The focus of the valuations must be upon the counselor in relation to clients lest the assessment become a clinical therapy experience. Although personal issues may arise in sessions, the process must remain supervisory and not therapeutic.

The counselor ought to have opportunities to evaluate the supervisor's performance, in an atmosphere that is open to criticism and free from sanctions.

The evaluations should be fair and well-balanced showing stagnation and growth.

Counselor Trait Profile

Circle the number on each line at the point where you see your counselor operating in terms of his/her job performance.

1	2	3	4	5	6	7	8	9	10
Autocratic (Makes decisions)									Encourages input from others
1	2	3	4	5	6	7	8	9	10
Judgmental Accusative									Nonjudgmental
1	2	3	4	5	6	7	8	9	10
Accepts ideas easily									Refuses to accept ideas
1	2	3	4	5	6	7	8	9	10
Makes clients feel relaxed, open									Makes clients feel defensive
1	2	3	4	5	6	7	8	9	10
Encourages dependence									Encourages independence
1	2	3	4	5	6	7	8	9	10
Acts consistently									Acts inconsistently
1	2	3	4	5	6	7	8	9	10
Eager to experiment with new ideas									Reluctant to experiment with new ideas
1	2	3	4	5	6	7	8	9	10
Readily available for help									Rarely available for help

1 2 3 4 5 6 7 8 9 10

Displays a sense of trust towards others — Displays a sense of mistrust towards others

1 2 3 4 5 6 7 8 9 10

Decisive — Indecisive

1 2 3 4 5 6 7 8 9 10

Treats others as equals — Treats others as inferiors

Present Job Skills Index

How satisfied are you with the way you carry out the various function of your job? Consider each of the following skills and indicate your degree of satisfaction with your efforts by checking the appropriate number, 1–5, with one being very satisfied, 3 being somewhat dissatisfied, and 5 being very dissatisfied.

1. Setting goals for self and others ____
2. Planning and organizing work ____
3. Designing work and methods ____
4. Organizing and directing others ____
5. Getting along with people ____
6. Proving counseling for members of staff ____
7. Delegating to others ____
8. Acting decisively with clients ____
9. Constructive listening ____
10. Effective communication with clients ____
11. Record-keeping ____
12. Understanding theories and conceptualizing the counselor role ____
13. Working with supervisor ____
14. Other (please specify) ____

Supervisor's Evaluation 1

Indicate next to each item your assessment of the counselor at the present time in relation to that item, with 1 being outstanding performance, 2 above average, 3 satisfactory, 4 poor, and 5 unsatisfactory performance.

1. Recognizes and disciplines own biases, prejudices, negative reactions to clients, etc. ____
2. Accepts limitations on his capacity and motivation and works with clients at their own tempo ____
3. Uses good judgment in determining what information needs to be obtained in a particular situation ____
4. Makes relevant inferences from data through appropriate application of theory ____
5. Achieves good balance in treatment between stimulating the client to act on his own behalf and, when necessary, making recommendations ____
6. Can identify and utilize appropriate strategies of intervention relevant to client needs ____
7. Understands latent and manifest communication in counseling ____
8. Case recordings are well organized and reflect the essentials of the case ____
9. Understand position in agency and appropriate channels for intraagency communication ____
10. Shows little need to defend herself against learning ____
11. Shows evidence of use of learning in subsequent client contacts ____
12. Is able to function as a productive, contributing member of staff ____

Supervisor's Evaluation 2

1. Is aware of own feelings in relationships and controls them so as not to impede the relationship ____

2. Establishes a relationship characterized by rapport, ease, and psychological safety ____
3. Able to communicate acceptance of wide variety of behaviors while not condoning unacceptable behavior ____
4. Able to obtain clear and accurate picture of problem situations with which client wants help ____
5. Able to organize and synthesize data in understanding client ____
6. Confirms, refines, modifies diagnostic formulation as appropriate ____
7. Able to identify community resources in client's behalf ____
8. Able to accept limited treatment goals without feeling immobilized ____
9. Facilitates communication in counseling sessions ____
10. Understands and responds to nonverbal as well as verbal communication in sessions ____
11. Recording reflects nature of interaction ____
12. Is constructive and appropriate regarding agency policy ____
13. Able to contribute constructive disagreement in supervisory sessions ____
14. Takes responsibility for establishing own learning needs ____

Supervisor's Evaluation 3

Indicate next to each item your assessment of the counselor at the present time in relation to that item, with 1 being outstanding performance, 2 being above average, 3 satisfactory, 4 being poor, and 5 unsatisfactory performance.

1. Attitude and motivation ____
2. Counseling skills ____

3. Conceptual functions: clarifying client's needs, and implementing treatment approach ____
4. Emotional accessibility: able to deal with feelings ____
5. Openness to feedback ____
6. Flexibility ____
7. Professionalism: able to separate personal issues ____
8. Self-awareness: able to recognize personal dynamics and cognitive picture of self ____
9. Empathy and honesty ____
10. Stress tolerance: able to accept anger and engage in necessary confrontations ____
11. Awareness of group process, roles and patterns of members, if applicable ____
12. Self-disclosure to others ____
13. Modeling behavior for clients ____
14. Techniques appropriate to clinical situations ____
15. Comments on counselor's performance, and recommendations for areas of need and skill development ____

SUPERVISOR'S EVALUATION 4

The following supervisor's evaluation is more detailed than the above, and focuses on the levels of skills of the counselor. The supervisor is to score the counselor based on her assessment of the counselor's present performance.

Performance

1. Attends sessions regularly and is punctual ____
2. Shows interest and attention ____
3. Is dependable in completing assignments ____
4. Is open to new ideas and contributes new ideas ____
5. Seeks feedback from and provides feedback to colleagues ____

6. Contributes to case discussions ____
7. Is able to question ideas discussed ____
8. Cooperates and is receptive to constructive criticism ____
9. Demonstrates an ability to synthesize material and to use it in her sessions ____

General Work Attitudes and Performance

1. Able to work with co-workers in the agency ____
2. Attitude of responsibility with patients and agency ____
3. Able to see her treatment as part of a multimodality approach, and to coordinate treatment with other caregivers involved with client ____
4. Able to maintain necessary safeguards to ensure confidentiality of clients and ethical standards for clinical practice ____

Performance in Competency Areas

1. Intake, including considerations of extent to which counselor gives clients opportunities to express their perceptions, obtains and records all information necessary for care, communicates hope and is friendly and understanding ____
2. Client assessment, including considerations of extent to which counselor records coexisting physiological and psychological conditions; can recognize types of clients, and stages of pathology; recognizes other illnesses as possible sources of problems; obtains information about major and minor illnesses adequate for referral; obtains detailed drug and alcohol history; provides an accurate diagnostic interpretation from client information; makes appropriate recommendations; can maintain appropriate

client records and reports; and can share evaluation findings with client and work through client reactions and resistances to this evaluation ____

3. Developing a treatment plan: has a written individualized plan for each client which includes specific steps to be taken by counselor and client and the rationale for the course of treatment; has plans which include long and short-term goals; and plans are revised systematically and periodically ____
4. Individual counseling: clearly communicates information about the problem of client; establishes a supportive, empathic relationship; helps patients understand their problems and patterns of coping with stress and need for mood-altering substances; can identify client's assumptive world (values); and can use counseling techniques to elicit feelings, facilitate self-understanding, and motivate the client ____
5. Group counseling: recognize and interpret attempts to structure group; reflects group affect; identifies avoidance of therapeutic tasks by intervention; reflects common fantasies in group; reinforces insight, mutual support, etc.; promotes catharsis in group; and defines and maintains group boundaries and rules ____
6. Family counseling: facilitates continuing communication among family members; utilizes a variety of techniques to promote growth and communication among family members; and involves members in resolving problems and shares each member's perspective ____
7. Referral services: has a relationship with persons who handle intake from other agencies which client might be involved with; and fol-

lows-up on services rendered via an appropriate tracking system ____

8. Crisis intervention: is patient but firm in setting limits with clients; is able to elicit necessary information for client to act; and handles physical violence appropriately ____
9. Knowledge of medications: knows effects and side effects of drugs used in treatment; and reports to medical staff on use and misuse of medications ____
10. Knowledge of alcohol/alcoholism: knows the physiological and psychological aspects of alcohol use and is familiar with detoxification procedures for substance abuse clients ____
11. Emergency medical care: recognizes signs of impending delirium tremens, hallucinosis, heart failure, seizures, toxic states, and knows when to act; and maintains contact with client and emergency staff after referral for services, follow-up to ensure that care has been given ____
12. Aftercare: establishes individualized follow-up programs with clients, including scheduled recontact times; and makes an effort to know clients' current situation and also anticipates future life stresses, and provides anticipatory support ____

Counselor Understanding of Treatment and Affective Qualities

1. Understanding of therapy, specially: able to conceptualize the therapeutic experience; able to identify his own assumptive system; able to justify therapeutic intervention; and able to understand the extent to which his personal feelings

and attitudes may be an impediment to treatment ____

2. Affective qualities of: empathy, respect, genuineness, concreteness, congruence, confrontation, self-disclosure, immediacy, potency, and self-actualization ____

General Impression of Counselor

Counselor's strengths ____________________

Counselor's weaknesses ____________________

Ranking of counselor in comparison with other staff ____________________

Specific plans to correct these weaknesses and build on strengths ____________________

Trainee's Learning Experience and Role Expectations

The process of becoming a counselor consists of at least three major stages: beginning, experienced, and mature. New supervisors tend to work with counselors in the first two stages, such as field placement or observation students. This stage ends when the trainee has acquired a rudimentary theoretical framework, some basic skills in counseling, and an introduction to client care.

Perhaps the most important factor to be dealt with in this stage is the trainee's anxiety. The anxiety is heightened by the misconception that he will destroy the client if he says or does the slightest thing wrong. This is termed the "spun-glass theory of the mind," held by many novice counselors.

Another source of stress for new counselors is the intensity and immediacy of the emotions of people in counseling. Trainees are often surprised and fearful when they discover they can elicit intense reactions that they do not know how to handle effectively.

The supervisor can help the new counselor deal with these stresses by instilling a sense of trust in the competency of the supervisor himself. If a supervisor has doubts about her own skills, it is difficult for her to deal with the trainee's fears. It is helpful for the supervisor to stress that mistakes are inevitable, and that she will be standing beside the counselor to aid when mistakes occur. Interventions by the supervisor are seen as providing useful information and feedback and not as disciplinary actions.

The experienced counselor has acquired a set of basic skills, and has, for the most part, overcome her anxiety about clients, and can function independently. She is capable of organizing treatment plans, and has gained a sense of professionalism, and responsibility. She, however, requires further training in order to gain experience with a variety of clinical situations, problems, and clients. She desires to learn specific treatment techniques and orientations. In the substance abuse field, many new counselors enter supervision looking for specific "tricks" without a basic knowledge and background in helping skills. It is the task of the clinical supervisor to inform counselors of the areas of need, the stages of their professional and personal development, and to set up learning goals in keeping with these strengths and weaknesses.

The tasks for the supervisor of an experienced trainee are somewhat different from those of the novice counselor. They involve sharpening, enhancing, and integrating the skills the person already possesses. The goals of the clinical supervisory sessions are fairly specific. The supervisor functions more as a consultant and technician to the counselor. The supervisor must develop some flexibility of style in order to allow room for the skills and maturity of the counselor to surface.

Some initial supervisors are awed by their positions of power and responsibility. Having chafed under authority figures themselves, and having endured the often arbitrary quality of evaluation, supervisors sometimes find themselves in conflict when put in such positions of authority.

It can also be disturbing to realize for the first time they are the expert, the one to whom others turn for security, clarity, and ideas. These role expectations are difficult. It is necessary to learn to say "I don't know," or "I don't understand that either." Time, however, seems to be the only answer to avoiding these pitfalls. The supervisor learns to develop anticipatory strategies to let people know what to do and what is expected of them.

For the third stage of counselor development, the mature counselor, the supervisor serves as an ally, coresource person, and a peer who is able to share ideas and information. Although the supervisor must maintain her position of power and responsibility for the care of the unit, when supervising a mature counselor the person can be far more open, and work together as coequals. This stage is rarely reached however for a number of reasons: Most mature counselors find themselves promoted to supervisor roles. Either counselors or supervisors are threatened by an equal relationship, and clinical supervisory sessions begin to become less and less frequent until eventually they are nonexistent. Most mature counselors are high-functioning individuals with many responsibilities themselves in the agency, thus making scheduling of clinical supervisory sessions difficult.

Chapter 6

PROCEDURES FOR CLINICAL SUPERVISION

PRINCIPLES OF ADULT LEARNING

The clinical supervisor functions as administrator, supporter, and educator. The first step in the educational process is to discern the personal, emotional, and professional needs of the staff. The supervisor must take an inventory of these needs prior to the beginning of training. Consideration of the needs as outlined by Maslow and conducting a discrepancy analysis are components of these needs assessments.

Individualized learning is essential to the clinical supervisory process. This involves making an educational diagnosis of each counselor's adult learning styles. The supervisor should observe the counselor's use of the participation in supervision, his motivational levels, his flexibility and rigidity in growth, his preparedness and attitudes. Some learn best in highly structured situations, others in loosely structured ones. All of these factors play a part in the supervisor's needs assessments of each counselor.

Since teaching is, according to Webster, "showing how to

do something, to provide knowledge," and learning is a process of gaining knowledge and skills, the clinical supervisor should abide by certain maxims for effective teaching.

RULE I: Counselors learn best when they are motivated to do so. There are a number of supervisory techniques that can motivate staff.

1. The content of the material to be taught in supervision must be carefully explained to counselors.
2. Supervisory sessions must address the counselor's needs. This involves both conducting needs and discrepancy analysis on each counselor, and demonstrating to the counselors how their need for autonomy will be met via supervision.
3. By developing a sense of commitment to the agency, counselors can be motivated to learn. Peer identification is a strong motivator for training which can be utilized in developing a positive learning environment.
4. Stimulation of the counselor's dissatisfaction with his performance serves as a motivator for learning. Supervisors can confront staff with the discrepancy between what they are doing clinically and what they want to be able to do. Supervisors can arouse stress in staff by breaking through defenses and pointing out rationalizations. Counselors are motivated to learn only when they like or respect the supervisor. A negative relationship can block the learning process. Identification with the supervisor heightens the counselor's motivation to learn.

RULE II: Counselors learn best when their energy is devoted to the learning process. Feelings like anxiety, stress, failure, threat, uncertainty and guilt inhibit learning.

1. Staff and supervisors must understand and agree on such issues as time, place, roles, duration of sessions, expectations, learning goals and objectives, cur-

riculum, requirements, and limitations. The philosopher Seneca wrote, "No wind is favorable if you do not know your destination."

2. Counselors must be permitted to arrive at their own solutions to problems in a nonparental atmosphere. The supervisor must be flexible in his goals and objectives for training. He should ask questions such as, "What do you think?" and "How do you feel about it?" The counselor should be encouraged to be an active, equal participant in the training in an interactional pattern of mutuality.
3. The supervisor must establish a climate that is accepting, safe, and secure; one that tolerates mistakes and failures. People must feel free to say, "I don't know." An atmosphere free of censureship and rejection must be established. Demands by both parties must be presented in a friendly, constructive manner, aiming to help, not hurt, each other. The supervisor must remember that he is the counselor's mentor, not tormentor.
4. Popularity is a seconday goal to learning for the supervisor. Errors and ignorances must be challenged and mistakes corrected in a constructive atmosphere. To do otherwise would be like giving an Eskimo ice in winter. Counselors become dissatified when supervisors are not sufficiently critical of the counselors' performance. A staff member must know what he is doing, and what needs to be changed.
5. The supervisor should build on strengths and not weaknesses. Strengths promote a sense of security, confidence, and comfort. Weaknesses provoke anxiety and stress. A contagious effect develops when the supervisor believes in the staff's abilities and skills. Strengths are enhanced by accepting that plateaus are inevitable and not all counselors learn at the same pace. The supervisor must consider each counselor's individual learning styles.

RULE III: Constructive and successful rewards enhance the learning process.

1. The objectives for learning must not be set too high or beyond the staff's reasonable limits.
2. Discriminate praise is a successful motivator when given immediately following a specific therapeutic behavior. Praise given weeks after the event is poorly utilized.
3. Periodic stock-taking via formal evaluations are useful to provide a sense of growth and progress. They serve as motivators of behavior when done regularly and routinely.
4. Learning should be parceled out through clearly defined and attainable learning objectives, mutually discussed and agreed on by the supervisor and counselor. The material should be graded, moving from the simple to the complex, the concrete to the abstract, the practical to the theoretical.

RULE IV: Counselors learn best when they are actively involved in the learning process.

1. Counselors should be involved in setting the content and agenda for the supervisory sessions to ensure relevance to their needs.
2. Opportunities need to be provided to raise questions to the material discussed in sessions. The supervisor can augment the thinking of the counselor, one step behind him. The supervisor should not become authoritarian and directive, unless a specific need by a staff member necessitates such action. Opposing viewpoints ought to be permitted and encouraged in an accepting, open, and safe climate.
3. Experimentation, learning by doing, is the key to supervision. "Learning determines action, but successful action reinforces learning."

4. Material should deal with counselors' everyday clinical functioning. It should be comprehensive in scope and consistent with the philosophy of the agency. Extreme eclecticism is confusing to a novice counselor, especially for the nondegreed individual who is probably trying to establish his own theoretical roots.

   A particular philosophical approach to counseling (a specific weltanschauung and cosmology) is important for the supervisor to possess if she is to provide a coherent learning model. Discrete, unrelated details of behavior are difficult to assimilate without theoretical scaffolding which can provide a "unity behind the plurality of experiences." Bruner (1963) states that unless detail is placed into a structured pattern it is rapidly forgotten. However, whatever the theoretical framework of the supervisor, it must never be presented in a dogmatic, paternal fashion, and never "crammed down the throats of staff."
5. Repetition is the key to keeping counselors involved in the supervisory process. Comparisons, contrasts, differences, similarities, and repetitions of clinical practice should be presented by the supervisor. The content of the sessions must be so organized as to reinforce material at each meeting. Training ought to be sequential, continuous, and integrated with frequent summations of what is being learned. A sense of goal attainment should be sought.

Context and Content: Individual Clinical Supervision

The most frequent context for clinical supervision is the one-to-one, individual session, regularly scheduled at a mutually convenient time, and conducted in a place of privacy, free from interruptions. Supervisors make the mistake of believing that effective clinical supervision can be conducted "on the run" in the hallway between conferences. One form that this method takes is the "Trouble Shooter" supervisor who says, "let me know if anything goes wrong. Call me in cases of emergency—I'll be right there." Another form is the "hit and run" supervisor who says to staff, "I'll see you in the hall for a few minutes when my session is over." Finally, there is the "crutch" supervisor who says, "I'll help you get started until you can stand on your own feet. Let's talk about the problems briefly so you can get started."

Too few supervisors set time and place aside to allow for a comfortable atmosphere that is conducive to learning. Interruptions often interfere with sessions; "emergencies" always seem to arise around the time of the session. Designated places and times are essential. Coverage for the unit must be arranged prior to the session so both supervisor and counselor can be free from interruptions.

Informal, on-the-spot conferences can occur when crises arise. Yet, the supervisor should not allow sessions to become off-the-cuff. In unscheduled conferences both parties enter unprepared, with snap judgments and recommendations given. These sessions lack continuity and coordination. Live material is impossible to add to the discussion. The "may I see you for a quick minute" supervisory session is an inadequate substitute for scheduled sessions.

Based on the research on clinical supervision, the optimal length for individual sessions is 45 to 60 minutes. For group sessions, 90 to 120 minutes seems to be the point at which the sessions reach their highest point of productivity. Individual sessions longer than 60 minutes become counterproductive as time wears on.

Both parties must arrive at a mutually agreed upon contract of learning goals for the sessions. This contract can be formalized in writing, outlining the expectations for the sessions, the preparation required of both individuals, case reports necessary, and the desired format for the presentation of "live material," recommended reading, etc. Remedial study may be necessary to fill in the knowledge base gaps.

The teaching syllabus for the sessions should be prepared between the supervisor and counselor. Both should be expected to prepare for the sessions by reviewing their notes on the content to be discussed. Because of the nature of the alcoholism counselor, the supervisor must not demand too much outside reading, but to depend more on repetitive, personal discussions with the counselor. The worker's clinical experiences become the "textbook" for the sessions.

The counselor's written case record is the best source of material for sessions. However, "live material" via written case records is a "second hand" observation of the counselor's work and can be distorted by the misperceptions of the event by the selective memory of the counselor. This is especially the case with verbatims, case presentations, and other forms of transcribed, interpreted material.

Counselors do not always perceive, recall, or retell failures in their clinical approach. This does not mean that counselors intentionally falsify the record through these omissions. Rather, what occurs is a process of selective perception in the defense of one's ego to maintaing self-respect. There is no failing too big or too small that cannot be avoided. Thus, clinical supervision based solely on the written or verbal report provides at best a retrospective reconstruction which is subject to serious distortions.

However, these distortions of the clinical event can be turned by a skilled supervisor into a learning experience to indicate the manner in which the counselor perceives the experience and desires to portray the event to the supervisor. The supervisor can provide a reflection of what is occurring and combine with "live material" such as audio visuals, direct observation, etc., to augment the present information. All case records inevitably contain some distortions. However, these distortions can become the content of the clinical supervisory experience.

The supervisor must know what actually occurred in the

counseling event and not what the counselor thinks or says occurred. Some form of live material of the clinical event is necessary to maximize the training experience. One method is for the supervisor to directly observe a counseling session conducted by the supervisee. (The client's permission is, of course, required, a step unfortunately forgotten in many agencies.)

Some feel that this procedure of direct observation interferes with the counseling session. Research has shown, however, this is not the case. An advantage of the supervisor sitting in on a session is that she can serve as a cotherapist, demonstrating her skills and serving as a role model for the counselor. Her clinical competency can be further displayed. Although the counselor may feel inhibited initially and may not feel able to participate freely and equally in the session, it has been demonstrated that the supervisee will eventually be able to become an active partner in the session. The clinical supervisory sessions are thus enriched as the supervisor is now able to evaluate his own performance.

To utilize this cotherapy model, the supervisory relationship must be strong with a sense of openness on the part of the counselor and supervisor. The latter must be able to take risks. Throughout this process, it must always be remembered that the "bottom line" for any supervisory procedure is the well-being of the client. No technique should be employed that interferes with the client's health.

Another supervisory technique is the use of a one-way mirror, thus minimizing intrusions during the counseling session. Interviews can be observed by the supervisor and other counselors without being seen or heard. However, there are a number of problems with this form of live material: Anyone who has ever sat for hours in a darkened room behind a one-way glass knows that sleep can replace interest. No permanent record of the clinical event is available for later study and discussion. One-way mirrors can distract the client; "Who is behind there looking at us?" Both counselor and client can be uncomfortable.

These drawbacks have been overcome through the use of

other forms of technology. The most frequently used medium in the field is videotape via an unobtrusive camera in a control room behind a one-way glass, or inconscpicuously placed in a corner of the counseling room. Wide angle and zoom lenses, rotating and/or multiple cameras, superimposition, and split screening techniques provide an astonishing range of possibilities for live material recording. However, this technology has gone further ahead than the capabilities of the supervisor or staff to properly utilize the equipment. Few clinical supervisors have the faintest notion of how to run videotape machines and how to maximize their potential as a training tool. Often, thousands of dollars on equipment are wasted on poorly trained supervisors whose mechanical expertise is limited to knowing how to turn the videotape on and off. Aside from technical issues, supervisors often have no training in the pedagogical use of the equipment.

This point is highlighted in the experience of the author who observed the utilization of the audiovisual equipment at one of the best endowed counselor training centers in the United States. The $250,000 videotaping system, with seven consoles and three separate viewing screens per console and immeasurable capabilities was limited by the technological ignorance of the supervisors. Even amid such technology the supervisory process was confined by the problems of retrieving the right tapes for the right sessions when needed, of recalling what session was being taped, what stages of treatment were being observed, and the limitations of the supervisor in processing the recorded content. Thus, before one dreams of a mini-NASA center with consoles of audiovisual equipment, the supervisor should invest in a course on the effective operation and use of the equipment in the clinical supervisory process.

This is not to minimize the value of videotape equipment. It provides a complete, reliable, and vivid portrayal of the counseling event. It allows the supervisor and counselor a chance to discuss the event so that the observations and suggestions of the supervisor become more relevant and appropriate.

Videotaping recreates the setting and event, and does not lie. It does not distort the actual clinical event.

Videotape replay provides the opportunity of seeing the counselor in action. The discrepancy between the counselor's self-image and his actual behavior is perfectly clear on the replay. Covert and overt behaviors are displayed.

Self-supervision can occur via videotape replay. Second looks and multi-level message integration are possible in a neutral setting. The tape speaks for itself, with little need for comment by the supervisor. Every smile, body movement, grimace, eyebrow move, frown, verbal, and nonverbal message is recreated. The counselor has the opportunity to recreate his feelings and relive the experience while observing the tape. The key to maximizing the potential of this equipment is found in the supervisor's skill in pointing to the counselor's verbal and nonverbal actions and deriving conclusions from these perceptions.

Tapes should be played, replayed, and played again. There should be a discriminating use of key sections of the session. Too many supervisors make the mistake of playing through whole tapes without sufficient interruptions for comment. Too much material is almost as bad as too little. The supervisor should focus on various components of the clinical event, the physical setting, the verbal and non-verbal messages. Turning down the audio and watching the video only is a way of looking at non-verbal cues. Verbal cues can be examined by turning off the video. Comparisons can be made between the perceptions of both messages.

A retrospective examination of the counselor's work is provided through videotaping. Provocative questions can be asked by the supervisor regarding omissions in the session. The supervisor can ask the counselor to describe his feelings during the session; the body movements of counselor and client can be translated; the thinking of both can be reconstructed.

However, far too few small substance abuse agencies can afford to purchase costly videotaping equipment. The supervisor often has to settle for audio equipment, a small percentage of the cost of a video machine ($100 vs. $2,000). Audio recorders, although not as flexible and graphic, can provide interesting and helpful live material for clinical supervisory sessions. It is a medium that should not be excluded from the supervisor's repertoire because it is not as "sexy" as video equipment.

One problem with audiovisual equipment is the resistance of counselors to taping. All sorts of excuses are used so that sessions do not get recorded: "The client would not give his permission," (he never asked the client); "Next week," (which never comes); "I do not know how to run the equipment," (try reading the manual); and, "This is a very sensitive case I am working with and taping will interrupt the therapeutic process," (it will interrupt the counselor's anxiety level.). Once a counselor does tape a session, he will be far more favorable to the process. The "ice breaking" is key; he finds that taping is not used as a tool against him. Besides, who does not like seeing themselves on television.

Another problem is that taping provides direct access to the supervisor's performance as well. There is pressure for the supervisor to tape a counseling session as a training tool. Although threatening to the supervisor, this can be a very positive role-modeling experience. If the supervisor already feels threatened by her position, if she has doubts about her abilities, she may resist taping sessions. However, this problem must be overcome if the supervisor is to survive in that position.

Thus, live material of the counseling event, via verbatims, coleadership of counseling sessions, videotaping, one-way mirrors and direct observation of sessions, are essential to the supervisory process. Without these materials, supervision becomes a second-hand recall of the clinical event. Constructive criticism of the counselor's skills and practice is limited by the creative imagination and memory of the recaller. Supervision without live material is "post facto" teaching, an examination of the counselor's activities in retrospect, in a vacuum. It involves the counselor in a systematic, intensive, and explicit analysis of his work. Through the use of this material, supervision becomes a process of self-observation and systematic review of the counselor's work.

A number of other tools are available to the supervisor, such as extramural, supplementary readings. These can be assigned to the staff between sessions. Relevant passages from texts can be recommended to supplement the material discussed at sessions.

Another supervisory tool is the use of role plays and simulation games. These obviously are best done in small groups, but can also be effective in individual sessions. They are problem-centered, and action-oriented, and address adult learning styles in that they offer vicarious, dramatic portrayals of clinical issues.

However, a number of rules must be applied to the use of role play:

The role-playing situation must be readily improvisable and clearly presented to the players. The nature of the problem, the roles, the approach of the counselor, the clinical setting must be clearly stated in setting the stage for the role play.

Role-playing techniques should be used after a sense of trust and security has been established between counselors and supervisor.

In the initial supervisory sessions the supervisor should volunteer to play the more difficult and threatening role of the counselor. A positive role model is demonstrated. Risk taking in the sessions is thus encouraged.

Frequent use of briefer role-play vignettes provide a good introduction to lengthier role plays. Experiential sessions using these techniques can be exciting and challenging and can serve as a potent learning medium.

A final approach in clinical supervision is the use of gestalt and other psychotherapeutic techniques. These methods serve as means of breaking through client/counselor impasses. An illustration of the use of gestalt techniques in supervision is presented in Chapter 7.

Context and Content: Group Clinical Supervision

For counselors, group clinical supervision is one of the most effective learning mediums. In contrast to other group activities, such as staff meetings, in-service training sessions, and grand rounds, the purpose of group clinical supervision is to implement the responsibilities of supervision as defined previously. It provides a structured formal group with specific tasks and agendas. Although there may be some variation in time depending on the number of counselors and the administrative problems associated with convening a group of staff members in one place at one time, the optimal time for group clinical supervision seems to be 90 minutes.

The size of the group may vary but the preferred number of group members seems to be from this author's experience, four to five. Groups can be heterogeneous in composition, with other staff included. This adds to interdisciplinary cross-fertilization and the integration of various job functions into a homogeneous process. Other determinants for group composition are the concerns of various counselors, their training needs, job responsibilities, administrative issues such as scheduling, case assignments, etc. However, whether or not the group is heterogeneous or homogeneous in composition, group growth should inevitably occur.

For substance abuse counselors, group clinical supervision is an excellent medium to experience group interactions and processes. Group therapy is one of the most effective therapeutic methods in the field. Thus, group clinical supervision provides an exciting learning arena for counselors as well.

Advantages of Group Supervision

The advantages of group supervision are numerous. It saves staff time and effort as compared to individual supervision. These findings were made by Sales and Navarre (1970) and Kaslow (1972). A number of teaching methods can be utilized, such as peer supervision, debates, audiovisual displays, role playing, simulation games, panel presentations, etc. Experiences of counselors with similar clinical problems can be shared. In group all of the staff becomes smarter than any one individual. Finally, counselors can view other staff members' clinical work and compare this with their own.

A greater variety of clinical concerns and therapeutic techniques can be presented in group supervision. The learning process becomes richer and more varied.

A group therapeutic milieu is established providing emotional support to the counselors. The group provides the staff with a sense of belonging, support, sympathy, group cohesiveness, professional identity, praise, and aid. Peer interaction is established. One counselor's problems become the group's problems. The individual counselor learns that his concerns are not unique. Failures may be reflective of different clinical events, a lesson that assists the counselor in depersonalizing his failures.

The interactions of group supervision facilitate greater inter- and intraunit exchange and coordination.

Individual sessions may also be threatening to some counselors. For them, group supervision is a less anxiety-provoking learning medium, where criticism from peers may be more readily accepted than from a supervisor. A sense of group safety is established. In individual supervision only two viewpoints are presented, and the "master's" opinions will generally prevail. In group supervision, there are many viewpoints presented, and the group opinion can carry greater importance. The individual in the group is more readily able to express his opinions.

The supervisor can observe the counselor in various dyadic

relationships and interactions. Further, the supervisor can serve as a role-model for interactional styles in the group.

Various roles can be played out in the group, such as someone being the supporter/enabler, another being the comforter/criticizer, etc. This enables the supervisor to intervene in the process filling a number of roles necessary for growth.

Disadvantages of Group Supervision

In addition to these advantages to group clinical supervision, there are a number of disadvantages. Detrimental group competition can begin and interfere with the learning process and counselor morale. Group approval and narcissistic fulfillment can become important in the group. Pathologic conflicts can be played out in supervision. The group can focus on its most vocal member and this may not meet the needs of each group member.

When new staff is added, it is difficult to incorporate these new members into the group process. The supervisor must deal with issues such as subgrouping, changes in interactional patterns, group cohesiveness, and role expectations.

The counselor can abdicate his responsibility for problem-solving and rely on the group to come up with solutions. Individual growth can be inhibited. The less vocal group member can "disappear into the woodwork" of the group.

The group can pressure an individual to conform to group norms, thus stifling individual creative growth.

The supervisor may lose control of the group sessions. The odds are five to one; the supervisor is outnumbered. He may find it hard to regain control of the content of the sessions. Leadership struggles may develop in the group.

In summary, however, the advantages outweigh the disadvantages of group supervision. An optimal approach seems to be to combine individual and group sessions for each counselor. The "curriculum" for training flows from individual to group to individual sessions. The supervisor must respond to individual counselor needs at various times and stages of the process. A combination of individual and group supervision provides a continuity of learning and corrects many of the disadvantages of both mediums.

Conducting a Group Session

How does the supervisor conduct a group session? What process is followed? Basically, the same procedures followed in conducting group therapy sessions are followed in group supervision sessions. This necessitates an awareness by the supervisor of group dynamics.

The most desirable physical arrangement for group supervision is a circle of chairs in a moderately sized room. Nonverbal messages ought to be possible in the physical arrangement of the room.

Group clinical supervision sessions must be regularly scheduled at a mutually agreed time. All group members must agree on the purpose of the sessions. The supervisor should always be the group leader, responsible for stimulating discussion, regulating group focus, directing group tasks, encouraging self-development and stimulation.

Audiovisual presentations of counseling sessions stimulate discussion. The tape can be stopped at significant junctions for group discussion of how the staff would handle the situation at that point. They can be asked to speculate on what should occur next in the clinical event.

The group should not be permitted to flounder with rhetoric and armless discussion that does not serve productive purposes. The clinical supervisor must maintain a relevant focus to group activities by dealing with the content in a problem-solving manner. The purpose must always be in the interest of learning.

It is useful for the supervisor to regularly summarize group process and content. The supervisor, though, must safeguard against overinvolvement in the group. The group members themselves must become their own watchdog, directing interactions and structuring group activities.

The group must take responsibility for regulating its own actions, amending the course of discussion, and maintaining the basic group functions. If the group fails to do so, the supervisor must intervene, mediating and preventing unnecessary conflict, controlling monopolies, and isolating individual group members from destructive interactions.

The content of group supervision sessions varies depending on the individual counselor and group needs. The group focus will be determined by the types of clients seen and the range of services provided. Each member's concerns can be addressed in group via case presentations and the utilization of live materials. It is most helpful if written transcripts of tapes and verbatims are completed prior to the session. They should be distributed to all group members to prepare for the session and to maximize the learning process and group discussion.

The curriculum for group supervision is the clinical presentation, i.e., the live material. It serves as the catalyst for discussion. At all times, though, the clinical material must be consistent with the group's goals and objectives and provide sufficient stimuli for discussion. The material must be relevant to the group as a whole. The supervisor should recapitulate the significance of the material when necessary and relate this to the counseling functions of the staff and the agency goals. The supervisor should move the discussion from the specific case focus to generic issues facing each counselor.

A precaution to supervisors in choosing live material for group presentation: the material should be previewed by the supervisor prior to group viewing. Far too many hours of staff time is wasted in viewing irrelevant or inaudible material which should have been screened out by a responsible supervisor.

Power issues and interactions should be dealt with by the supervisor in group whether they occur within or outside the group context. The supervisor should be aware of and deal with the patterns of both formal and informal staff relationships. Hidden agendas and undercurrents in the group must be brought to the group for discussion.

One approach to dealing with "power" issues in group is to conduct Tavistock-like seminars with staff. These seminars deal with the problem of effectively blending the "boss-supporter" roles of the counselor. During these sessions, the clinical supervisor plays an educator role, offering the counselor and the group a developmental model for organizing and analyzing group interactions. Videotaping of these sessions is ideal in processing the interactions. However, a word of caution is necessary: Tavistock techniques are powerful, intensive tools to be employed only by skilled leaders with background and training in their methods. In the hands of a novice supervisor who wishes to "play around" with these tools there is a danger of irreparable damage to staff.

Finally, the supervisor should summarize the activities and materials presented at each session and at other appropriate times in the group process. This involves the interpreting of key issues presented, and preparing the group for subsequent sessions. The end of the session should be planned from the beginning so the agenda can be accomplished within the designated time. Reasonable closure should be sought.

The clinical supervisor should attend to the "housekeeping" chores of the group, including the assigning of responsibilities for the next session. The supervisor should conclude sessions with some specific questions for the counselors to ponder and material for reading for the next meeting. These serve as transitions for subsequent learning.

Chapter 7

PROBLEMS IN CLINICAL SUPERVISION

Clinical Supervision vs. Personal Psychotherapy

The goal of supervision involves both personal and professional growth for the counselor. These are related and parallel processes. Counselors must confront the problem areas of their lives, and work through these problems. Self-awareness and personal growth enhance one's clinical endeavors. A counselor would be dishonest to himself if he did not admit that, at some time in his clinical supervision, he benefitted personally. However, if personal growth is an explicit goal of supervision, this should occur in the open, through a mutually agreed upon decision.

However, the balance between personal and professional growth can become precarious as the supervisory relationship becomes more of a psychotherapeutic rather than a supervisory process. Self-awareness is an important and necessary correlate for counselors. Unlike many other professions, in substance abuse counseling there is considerable interplay between one's personal and professional lives. This is especially true for the recovering alcoholic. Clinical situations can remind him of his own life experiences. In counseling, he may find himself reminded of his own life problems—parent-child conflicts, aging, marital problems, the recovery process itself, sexual conflicts, relapses— all of which can activate feelings and conflicts in the counselor. Thus, the clinical supervisor has the responsibility of helping the counselor understand himself, developing self-awareness, as well as teaching him about people, problems, places, and processes involved in counseling.

Some disciplines such as clinical psychology and psychoanalysis make it obligatory for the entry level worker to be involved in her own psychotherapeutic process outside of the training experience. Since such a requirement does not exist in the substance abuse field, except for the fact that the individual must be free from any dependency on substances, the clinical supervisory process is an essential medium for self-understanding.

Unfortunately, in the alcoholism counseling field there is almost a distain for counseling and psychotherapy for staff members. Agency personnel often act hypocritically by covering up personal problems among staff members that may inhibit and detract from the growth of clients. Clinical supervision seems to be one of the less threatening means for the development of counselor self-awareness.

It is a curious phenomenon at a time when employee assistance programs have been developed for the troubled worker that the mental health field has a tendency to shelter its own and to push personal problems among staff "under the carpet." It is hoped that problems will go away by themselves. Treatment program directors are hesitant to refer the troubled employee for counseling, even though they preach to industries and community groups the importance of identifying problems. The field speaks out of both sides of its mouth about the stigma of substance abuse and the embarrassment of our society about mental health problems, and yet is hesitant to confront its own personnel about problems. At times the field becomes the "blind leading the blind."

However, at what point does clinical supervision become "therapizing the therapist?" Resolving or avoiding the dilemma of being therapeutic while not engaging in therapy requires an adherence to some guidelines and limitations on the role of the clinical supervisor. *The focus of the clinical supervisory relationship must always be on helping the counselor to become a better worker, not necessarily a better person.* The supervisor's legitimate concern is with the professional activities of the counselor. There are no sanctions provided by her title to probe into the personal life of the counselor, unless it impacts upon the counselor's professional functioning. "How can I help you" is not the issue for the clinical supervisor; "How can I help you with your work" is. Ekstein and Wallerstein (1972) note "in supervision we aim at a change in the skills, a change in the use of the professional self while in psychotherapy we aim at changes which embrace the total adaptive functioning of the individual" (p.5).

Personal issues, feelings, attitudes, and countertransferences can be dealt with by the clinical supervisor. However, the focus of this interaction must ultimately return to the clinical functioning of the supervisee. It has been said that the supervisor is like a good hotelkeeper who does not care what goes on in the privacy of the individual's room as long as it does not disturb the other guests. All thinking and feeling is ultimately acceptable provided (a big "provided") it does not result in unacceptable professional behavior.

The clinical supervisor cannot tolerate destructive personal behaviors that may harm the image of the agency in the community. For example, criminal or overt sexual behavior is unacceptable. The professional image of the agency must be maintained at all times.

Thus, the clinical supervisor can be therapeutic in her role and can deal with self-awareness issues. However, "therapizing" the relationship suggests that the supervisor is entering areas of the counselor's personal life with no organizational sanction or authority. At times a counselor can seduce the supervisor into playing therapist with him. Such game playing must be avoided by the supervisor.

If in the course of the clinical supervisory relationship either party perceives the need to deal in a psychotherapeutic environment with intra- and interpsychic issues, it is the obligation of the supervisor to encourage the supervisee to seek out such assistance. It is appropriate for the supervisor to refer the counselor needing further intervention to an outside therapist for help.

Dealing With Resistance

Staff resistance is the most difficult problem for the clinical supervisor to deal with. Requests for live material must be repeatedly made. It is like "pulling teeth" to have work presented at group clinical supervisory sessions. These experiences can be frustrating and annoying for the supervisor. Resistance can be destructive to the operations of the agency, the internal politics of the staff, and ultimately, the quality of patient care. Thus, resistance must be dealt with by the supervisor as quickly and expeditiously as possible.

The first step in dealing with resistance is to recognize the sources of tension and stress for the staff. Supervision as an educational process implies change and a temporary shifting of one's equilibrium. It says that there are weaknesses and areas of need for growth. Although a counselor may consciously recognize the need for skill development, and may acutely sense his own deficiencies and limitations, he will resist the educational aspects of supervision and maintain the facade of clinical competency and superiority.

Further, supervision requires the counselor to deal with

emotional issues. He must confront himself, his feelings, attitudes, and emotions as well as his professional competencies. This can be threatening to the counselor.

The supervisor threatens the independence and sense of autonomy of the counselor. It implies the sharing of clinical responsibilities. In a field already characterized by ambiguities of goals and techniques, it is little wonder that the supervisee is threatened by questions to his privilege to do what his professional judgment suggests.

Research suggests that the clinical supervisory relationship activates tension and anxiety for counselors, (Ekstein and Wallerstein, 1972; Fleming and Benedek, 1966; Schuster, Sandt and Thaler, 1972). The supervisory relationship is intensive, individualized, and personal in nature. Transference, countertransference, and early developmental conflicts are involved in the relationship; a parent-child relationship may be evoked. These issues, however, must be dealt with if the supervisory relationship is to fully mature. This tension/growth dynamic in the supervisory relationship is desirable and inevitable, provided the supervisor is able to work through these issues.

The counselor can play a number of games to resist the supervisory process. The "I am not going to tell you so you will not be able to hurt me later" game is a common one. Inconsequential matters and trivia lacking depth are focused on as a means of avoiding important issues. Passivity throughout the supervisory sessions is another form of resistance. If the clinical supervisor attempts to give the impression that he is all-knowing, the groundwork for these games is laid. This is especially true for alcoholism and drug abuse agencies where the counseling staff may be nondegreed professionals, and the supervisor a degreed person wishing to convey the message to the staff that "I know how to counsel alcoholics. Listen to me."

The polarization of professionals vs. paraprofessionals, degreed vs. nondegreed counselors, recovered alcoholics vs. counselors who were never alcoholics, must cease lest the field tear itself apart internally. If one is a counselor, he is by definition a professional. It is the responsibility of clinical supervisors to discontinue this polarization and to begin to build a healthy interchange for all workers, recognizing the particular skills and assets each of us bring to our work.

Staff occasionally play the game "you may be a good psychologist, but you don't understand the alcoholic. You have not been there like I have." This is best played by a recovered alcoholic staff member and a nonalcoholic supervisor. "How can you provide insight to me since I already know more about 'drunks' than you? Therefore, I will resist clinical supervisory demands."

The clinical supervisor must be aware of the basis for the resistance and the games being played. The supervisor must deal with these issues. The first step in confronting resistance is for the supervisor to communicate her physical, administrative, and psychological availability and approachability. Staff barriers must be broken down. The counselor may chose not to discuss problems with the supervisor. He must be made aware, however, that the supervisor is available to help when the supervisee desires help. An "open door" policy is essential.

Second, the supervisor must communicate his confidence in the counselor. Both share common goals and objectives. Both are interested in the delivery of the highest quality of client care. To facilitate this, the supervisor may wish to share her own failings, feelings, and frustrations. When done carefully, the openness can become the cornerstone of a supervisor-supervisee relationship. A mutual sharing of feelings often helps to assure the counselor that the supervisor is human and approachable. Questions such as "how do you feel about . . . ?" or "you seem somewhat upset about . . . " are keys to beginning to grow together in an honest relationship. It is helpful for the supervisor to share with the counselor his failures as well as successes. It further reminds the supervisee that no one is free from errors. No one can set himself up as an authority in all clinical situations.

Most new workers feel a certain sense of incompetency.

This should be communicated by the supervisor to the novice counselor. Further, a sense of confidence in the counselor should also be conveyed, otherwise, the counselor would not even have been hired in the first place. The supervisor should provide the counselor with opportunities to experience success in her clinical functioning. Increasing opportunities for independent functioning should also be provided. Praise and commendation for good performance are often the best "resistance overcomer" in the supervisor's trick bag.

Words of encouragement such as "you really helped that client; good work," help to build a supervisor-counselor relationship. However, unwarranted praise is transparent and counterproductive. It is more a reflection of the supervisor's own anxiety and not praise of the counselor's work.

Interpretation is perhaps the most direct and mature method of dealing with staff resistance. The supervisee is confronted with his behavior and a direct discussion of the resistance ensues. The interaction is intensified and a deeper level of communication may be established.

An example of interpretation by a clinical supervisor may be: "I get the impression you are resisting supervision because you have put me on a pedestal. This may be your way of hiding from feelings. This may be typical of how you resist people—fear of intimate, personal contacts with me and others."

Most clinical supervisors are unable to directly confront supervisees in this manner. Thus, a more indirect, less threatening method may be used. Feedback is a less confrontative method, yet can effectively deal with resistance. It emphasizes the internal reactions of the clinical supervisor instead of the external response of the supervisee. The supervisor points out the trainee's behavior and associated feelings within himself. For example: "You seem to be asking me to give answers, yet I feel uncomfortable doing so when you can arrive at your own solutions."

Further, by clarifying and restating what the supervisor hears, discrepancies in the trainee's behavior are pointed out.

For example, the supervisor may say, "You are at a loss in this clinical situation, so much so that you would have me advise you. Yet, you also want to be able to arrive at your own answers. Am I getting two different messages?" These techniques may be valuable in dealing with resistance from staff.

Another technique in overcoming resistance is for the supervisor to demonstrate his own clinical competency. "Expert power" is a key in seducing the staff to respect the supervisor's skills and wisdom. Supervisors may be seen as "paper-pushers," administrators, removed from the needs of clients. Some may think that the supervisor has forgotten what it is like being a front-line counselor. By "taking the risk" of displaying himself in a counseling situation, the supervisor can demonstrate her own competency. It is helpful to have the staff observe the supervisor in practice via one-way screens, direct observation, tapes, videotapes, verbatims, etc. She may act as a cotherapist with the counselor in a session. She may present a tape of both a good and bad session which she conducted. The best builder of success in the clinical supervisory relationship is clinical success, demonstrated in the observation of the supervisor's own practice.

The supervisor must be willing to share his own feelings, strengths, and weaknesses. As staff sees the skills of the supervisor, they will be more open to accept the supervisor's advice, criticism, and feedback. *Do not expect the staff to do something that you yourself are not willing to do.*

It is most helpful for the supervisor to carry a caseload, however small, as a means of demonstrating his own clinical skills and concern for clients. He becomes more than an administrator, removed from the needs of patients. He must be willing to "get his hands dirty" particularly in the substance abuse field. He must be willing to handle the hostile, intoxicated patient, vomiting on the steps of the agency. To look helplessly about, calling for the help of a counselor is to alienate the staff.

Another step in dealing with resistance is to clarify the lines of authority. "It's not my job, man," is the message that needs to be clarified. The "pudding concept of authority" is a factor here, which has been discussed in other chapters.

The supervisor must be consistent and persistent in her demands of the staff. Policies and obligations should be universally applied to all staff and not simply in problematic areas and with certain staff. The supervisor should continue in his demands and not equivocate at the first sign of resistance.

Finally, the supervisor must carefully assess each of the following questions about the staff:

Is the manifest resistance a sign of arrogance, aggression, dependence, etc.?

What are the problem-solving skills of the staff?

To what extent do personality problems play in the resistance?

What character deficits impede learning?

Is self-preservation an issue for the staff?

Is learning sought primarily to gain status rather than skills?

Is inductive or deductive learning more helpful for the staff? (Deductive is moving from the general to the specific. Inductive is moving from the specific to a series of similar situations involving relevant generalizations.)

Which counselors are slow learners and may be threatened by the "data dump" of information presented?

Does the staff understand their job functions?

Are company/agency policies and procedures understood and agreed upon by all staff?

Is the counselor capable of complying with his job responsibilities?

Is there a difference of understanding between the supervisor and staff in their interpretation of agency policies? For example, in the minds of staff, protecting the rights of clients may mean not submitting live materials for sessions. Does the staff view this as breaking confidentiality?

In sum, staff resistance can be overcome by a perceptive and patient supervisor who takes appropriate corrective action when needed.

Game Playing

Staff resistance is often played out in a series of games involving both counselor and supervisor. A whole repertoire of games can be played throughout the supervisory relationship.

"Him against us" is best played by a recovered alcoholic staff and a nonalcoholic clinical supervisor. "Let us do what we were hired for, to counsel. Why do you hassle us with administrative details? It keeps us from having time to see clients." Since administrative demands are with us always, this game can be played at most times (Kadushin, 1976).

The supervisor can feed into this game if he has unpleasant memories of administrative hassles. He may also have problems because he has never established in his mind his own role as part of the administrative staff.

"I'll stroke your back if you do mine," is a game that uses flattery as a lever to inflate the supervisor's ego. Everyone likes to hear how great he is as a supervisor. "I have learned so much from you," can melt the anger of almost anyone. "How can you place demands on me when I am being so nice to you?" This is emotional blackmail.

Further, by changing the focus of the supervisory relationship, another resistance game can be played. "Help me" is the script of this game. If one feels messianic anyway and wants to heal all, this is an especially valuable game for a staff member to play. One's self-image is flattered by the game; one needs to be needed. Yet, following the request for help is the plea, "How can you make demands from a poor struggling soul like me?"

Another redefinition game is, "I'm your friend. Don't criticize me." Transferences and countertransferences may be utilized in establishing friendships. "Let's have lunch together," "How about coming to our house for dinner," or "Want a ride home? It's out of my way, but I'd be happy to do it for you," are all variations on this theme. However, to be an intimate, a friend, also means to be less critical and judgmental. Staff will often try to become peers with supervisors. When this occurs, the distance needed to be critical and objective is lost, and the supervisory relationship develops a terminal case of atrophy.

"I know as much as you do, you are not so smart," is a variation on this game. "Have you read the latest issue of the Quarterly Journal on Alcohol Studies (or Psychology Today, etc.)." Events in supervisory sessions will remind the counselor of something she read in a scholarly text. "You have read that, haven't you . . . ?" The supervisor is being blackmailed, for rather than admitting his ignorance, he nods his head, and begins a counterproductive, deceptive relationship. The power balance has now shifted (Kadushin, 1976).

In the substance abuse field, this game is best played with the following script: "Oh, so you are not a recovering alcoholic," or "Too bad you are a recovering alcoholic." In the former script the distance is created, power and clinical competence deflated by letting all parties know that the supervisor cannot really understand the alcoholic client because "he has never been there. He is not like the rest of us." Therefore, the supervisor is somehow not as clinically competent. This is compounded if it has been some time since the supervisor has dealt directly with clients.

Older staff will allude to their age, and thus know more than the younger supervisor, even if some of that time was spent in an alcoholic stupor. Younger staff will hint at their greater understanding of the problems of the youth. After all, he has played with other "harmful substances," the supervisor of course never really knowing what that means, but may be too intimidated to ask. The married counselor will really know about marriage counseling and hint at the lack of knowledge and understanding of the single supervisor. Conversely, the recovered alcoholic supervisor may be "put down" by the nonalcoholic staff because he is probably "brain-damaged" anyway. This variation may be very subtle and often unspoken.

Black street counselors can expand on the game by playing "I know where it's at, honky." A profusion of four-letter words and street talk aids in this game. The extent to which this game is played is determined by the degree of discomfort and loss of composure displayed by the supervisor. The supervisor can forfeit his role by his bougeois and puritanical posture. Obviously, the supervisor cannot be effective because she is uncomfortable in dealing with "the real world." By her inability to confront the counselor when this game begins the supervisor contributes to the destructive interaction.

Another tactic is to involve the supervisor in a profusion of irrelevant issues and crises. Questions and problems of interest to the supervisor are introduced, thus allowing for an endless monologue on the subject by the supervisor. The supervisee can "turn off and allow the supervisor to do his number." Critical issues are thus avoided. The supervisor's narcissism is satiated.

A variation on this theme is to admit failings and mistakes at the onset, flagellate oneself, and act contritely. "How can you be critical of me now?" Support and reassurance is needed, when, in fact, a game of avoidance is being played. The "little lost lamb" and "What more can I do except what you tell me to do," games can be added to this theme. The supervisor becomes responsible for the action and mistakes of the supervisee. The supervisor is in a position of defending his advise on the case. By appealing to other authorities, ("Dr. X says. . . .") the supervisor's authority is questioned (Kadushin, 1976).

In addition to supervisee games, the supervisor can play games of her own, because of her anxieties about her position, her uncertainty about her own clinical competencies, the hierarchical structure of the agency, her power and authority, and her needs to be liked and accepted by all staff. Because supervisors feel distant from staff, the supervisor is tempted to play games to avoid problems.

"Therapizing the therapist" is a favorite game of supervisors. Counselors' behavior is obviously indicative of some maladjustment, particularly of the sort one learns in college Psychology 101. Counterproductive and inappropriate supervisory relationships can thus be established.

"M.S.W.'s know better," is a supervisor's version of the one-up-manship game. This game is even better played if one possesses a Ph.D., with the ultimate player being an M.D. (psychiatrist). In this game, as in the alcoholic–nonalcoholic game, the supervisor establishes his unquestioned authority on the basis of academic qualifications rather than clinical competency.

Another theme is "I'm so overburdened with responsibilities," or "How can you demand a minute of my precious time?" Last minute reports and special meetings aid the supervisor in canceling supervisory sessions. "We will reschedule it when I have more time" (which is probably never). If the supervisor feels inadequate, or is basically lazy, this is an excellent game. However, the supervisor's resistance to work at the supervisory relationship will inevitably be transmitted to staff.

Other words to use in this game are "If we only had more time," or "I am doing all of these things for you; you do want that pay raise next year don't you?" These words are best said as the supervisor rushes out the door to another "important meeting." "After all I do for you," is the message that is communicated.

Supervisors with delusions of grandeur will wish to create proteges in their own professional image. Staff is brainwashed into accepting "his" philosophy, rather than arriving at their own concepts and approaches. The supervisor is one to be imitated rather than identified with. When the counselor succeeds, the supervisor succeeds, and his messianic needs are met. Staff becomes an extension of the supervisor. Autonomy, creativity, and individuality are lost in this process.

Although many agencies in the substance abuse field develop their own individual approach to the treatment of clients, it is inappropriate for all agency personnel to conform to that philosophy, speaking, acting, eating, and sleeping with identical words, movements, and actions. Identical expressions and mannerisms are dull and do not allow for individualism and autonomy.

Another game played by supervisors is to focus solely upon the client and not on the counselor in relation to the client. The supervisor becomes interested only in clinical care and not clinical supervision.

The "I'm not going to expose myself" game is played by supervisors who feel insecure about themselves and their clinical knowledge. One's ignorance and insecurities are best not exposed. Small doses of information and "pearls of wisdom" can be passed out just enough to maintain one's status.

Supervisors also assume, at times, too much responsibility for the actions of staff. Errors are not permissible because they reflect the failings of the supervisor. Undue responsibility for all actions of staff is displayed.

These are a few of the games that can be played by supervisors and counselors. The obvious question is how to avoid or stop playing these games. Because supervisors are integrally involved in the games, it is difficult, if not impossible, for the supervisor to simply state that she will no longer play. Further, game playing can be an unconscious process, one which she is unaware of. To stop playing is to be willing and able to give up the self-serving advantages of the games, to be open to hostility, and able to deal with staff anxiety. She must be clear in her own authority and role, and confident in her own clinical and supervisory skills. It may be necessary for the supervisor to explore with someone outside of the immediate situation inter- and intrapsychic issues related to the game playing.

Kadushin (1976, p.252) writes, "In declining other games the supervisor denies himself the sweet fruits of flattery, the joys of omniscience, the pleasures of acting as therapist, and the gratification of being well liked. She incurs the penalties of an open admission of ignorance and uncertainty and the loss of infallibility."

Open confrontation is another method of dealing with game playing and staff manipulations. By bringing to light and demonstrating his awareness of the processes underway, the supervisor can state that he is unwilling to play any further. This should be done in a manner that does not embarrass or threaten the staff. The following prescription should be used in confronting staff: *Confrontation = a dose of timing + a large measure of compassion and understanding + a measure of how much confrontation is appropriate + a knowledge of one's staff.*

With this prescription, when given in proper amounts, the supervisor will be able to deal with staff's destructive behaviors and game playing as well as learn to resolve his own game playing.

Further Counselor–Supervisor Problems

Clinical supervision occurs within the context of a client–counselor–supervisor relational system. Occasionally, the clinical supervisor may find himself observing a symmetrical neurotic pattern between the patient and the staff member. Counseling can become unconsciously collusive, entwined in issues such as sexuality and transference. The supervisor must notice these patterns and confront the counselor with his behavior. The situation becomes more complicated when the symmetry is in the nature of style, not content, which may be unseen, unrecognized, and pervasive of the counselor's overall performance. For example, if the patient and the counselor are neurotically obsessional, counseling can become countertherapeutic. If the two are manipulative, the potential is there for intricate power maneuvers. The supervisor must deal with these issues through the use of live materials aiding the counselor to recognize her role in the process.

Counselors can find themselves involved in complementary neurotic patterns with clients, when the behavior of both exacerbates the behavior of each other resulting in a fascinating, nontherapeutic escalation. For example, a substance abuse counselor, because of a neurotic need to become overinvolved with the needs of clients, can find himself trapped by clients who wish to have a fused relationship with him. Blocks in the counseling process can be created. It is the responsibility of the supervisor to confront the counselor with this behavior.

Counselors also tend to distort their perceptions of the client. The counselor can form a pattern of distortion with all clients, such as responding to particular patients on the basis of age, race, gender, or socio-economic status. The recovering alcoholic counselor can condemn the behavior of his clients because they are not doing it the way he did. Male counselors can look down on the female alcoholic patient because of the stigma and stereotypes of women and alcohol. Poorer clients may be treated as "bums" whereas richer clients are treated as "sick people," especially as long as their Blue Cross coverage lasts. Distortions by counselors represent an important dynamic in the staff member's professional and personal life. If the counselor resists recognition of these distortions in the clinical supervisory sessions, the issues are probably dynamically important to the counselor and as such are likely to be played out in counseling.

Group supervision sessions are helpful in consensually validating or correcting the supervisor's perceptions of such distortions. If the behavior is numerous, pervasive, and nonresistant to change in the supervisory context, personal therapy outside of the work setting may be required. The supervisor has the responsibility to the patients to ensure that the counselor does get such help. Another short-term method is for the supervisor to assign the counselor to other cases. This approach, though, merely recapitulates the situation with other clients. If the problems remain pervasive, it may mean that the counselor should not be retained in that clinical role.

The counselor is not alone in having to deal with issues that may interfere with his functioning; the clinical supervisor also encounters job-related tensions requiring a change in behavior and attitude. He may find himself in an unfamiliar role as a supervisor, with expectations and responsibilities that need to be clarified. This is especially true for the nondegreed supervisor, working on his second career after years of drinking. He may have little or no formal training in supervision. Clinical supervision is different from the form of supervision he may have formerly experienced in the business world. New roles and relationships need to be established; new powers bestowed. He may experience tension and anxiety in this process.

As a counselor prior to being promoted to the supervisory role, he experienced personal satisfaction. The interpersonal relationships with clients were probably the reason for entering the field. Seeing lives changed in counseling was stimulating and rewarding. Now, however, he must give up some of that enjoyment, and stimulation and find other sources of reinforcement.

The novice supervisor must, at this point, examine his own practice and conceptualize on it for teaching purposes. He may or may not have the capacity for doing this. But, he must be able to articulate what it is he is doing with clients and why.

He must also deal with the conflicts of being a member of the administration, "joining the establishment." He may have resented the administration when he was a counselor. This is further complicated if the supervisor finds himself relating to staff with similar backgrounds and experiences. He may find himself in the midst of role conflicts, and at times personally at odds with his former friends on the staff. Peer relationship status is lost; social distances may form; and an atmosphere of formality may develop. His friends will become reluctant to share substantive issues with him as they did before.

New peer relationships must also be formed with other decision makers. The first time a new supervisor attends a unit chiefs meeting or administrative staff meeting can be frightening. Given all of these issues, the new supervisor must also deal with added responsibilities, work pressure, and clinical authority.

The supervisor may be anxious about her role of providing assistance, support, and "answers" to staff members. "I don't know what to say to staff about this client." Feelings of inadequacy may develop; an attitude of incompetency may grow. He now feels that he must be a question-answerer rather than a question-asker.

In some cases, problems may result from the "pudding" concept of authority wherein he is uncertain of his tasks, responsibilities, and powers. A clear job description may be lacking. The supervisor may flounder about looking for direction in a position that lacks definition. Limitations may be imprecise and responsibilities expansive.

Additional stress can be created by the nature of his being: female supervisors may find themselves with an all male staff who resent working for a woman. Younger supervisors may be rejected by older staff, and vice versa. Nondegreed supervisors may be looked down upon by degreed staff. A nonrecovered supervisor may find himself doubly separated from staff by not being one of them, and also being "the boss." Cultural gaps may exist as well: a white supervisor may be rejected by a black counselor because he cannot really understand the problems of the black alcoholic client. The reverse situation can contradict the positional authority in the usual social arrangement pattern.

Finally, problems for the supervisor may result from the following:

Administrative chores that the supervisor views as "red tape," unnecessary detail work, time-consuming bureaucratic reporting may become arduous tasks.

Decision making may be an unfamiliar role for the supervisor, especially if clearly defined programatic procedures and policies are absent.

Evaluating staff and making administrative decisions about employees may be difficult for the new supervisor.

Exercising administrative authority may be difficult for him.

Problems can result from the tendency to become a therapist to a former peer.

However, the first step in dealing with these problems is to realize that they are inevitable. They can be dealt with quickly at an early stage of the process. The other steps to resolving these problems are discussed throughout this chapter.

One key to resolving these problems is found in the proper matching of students with supervisors based on a number of factors;

Congruence of theoretical orientation.

Elimination of barriers to effective learning by pairing types of students with types of supervisors. The supervisor must have a sense of the various tasks of each trainee. Some supervisors are best suited to work with novice counselors, some with expert students.

Supervisor's attitudes towards different types of clients. Some are more comfortable with bright, verbal, neurotic clients; some with detoxifying patients; some with severely disturbed clients.

The needs of the supervisor. Some supervisors need to be admired, others need challenging. Those seeking respect should not be paired with competitive, challenging trainees.

Covert and overt agendas in supervision. Some supervisors may need to "convert" counselors to their therapeutic style. Some may be seeking to instill in counselors certain values. Some students may be seeking critical supervisors to justify their work.

How supervisors and counselors handle silence. Different trainees respond in various ways to supervisor silence. This may be perceived as sharing interest, or as disinterest, hostility, analytical behavior, and withholding information.

Directiveness by both parties. New students tend to want advice given to them. Later counselors see directiveness as authoritarian, controlling behavior.

Gender. Supervisors respond differently with males and females. Studies have indicated that supervisors tend to distance themselves more from female counselors and are less personally involved in the career goals of women staff members. Of course, the converse may also occur where inordinate interest is expressed in a female counselor by a male supervisor, or vice versa.

If care is taken in pairing up supervisors and counselors according to the above variables, many of the problems of supervision outlined in the preceding paragraphs can be avoided.

Confidentiality, Professionalism, Ethical Practice, and the Rights of the Counselor and Client

Epstein (1970) once wrote, "One of the principal reasons which makes the eradication of quackery forever impossible is to be found in the fact which finds expression in the proverb, 'Stupidity is a hardy perrenial.' " Such is especially so for the issues of professionalism, confidentiality, and ethical practice.

One learns to speak of not having a job but of being a member of a profession. Health care professionals, such as physicians, psychologists, social workers, etc., strongly identify with what they do, their status, functions, and responsibilities, all of which are an extension of their self-concept.

Clinicians have a sense of belonging to a professional group, and identify with that group's actions, code of behavior, and professional image. As an example, physicians identify with the Hippocratic Oath which assures the "outside world" of therapeutic responsibility. The counseling field, however, has been slow to develop this professional identity and code of behavior. A sense of magic still pervades the field. The writings in the past have sounded vaguely charletanistic, with doubts about what it is that counselors really do. Yet a facade of professional self-awareness was presented to the public.

This identity crisis may have been due in part to the question of whether counselors have the right to counsel; of whether it is a transgression of the rights of medicine. Counselors have suspected that they were somehow doing something wrong. This resulted in insular behavior precipitated by a paranoia that in fact they were transgressing on someone else's territory. Psychologists, social workers, and counselors had a sense of being torn by multiple purposes, poorly defined objectives, a lack of paradigms to determine their actions, and a lack of institutional alliance. The bottom line for the counseling field is to admit to the other professions and to itself that it is a young science, a new profession, without the answers, but with a clearly defined purpose and code of behavior.

One of the fundamental principles of counseling (and one rarely adhered to by alcoholism and drug abuse counselors) is that of confidentiality. For the sake of the client, the counselor is expected to hold in confidence what she hears, sees, or otherwise discovers about the client. The success of the counselor hinges on the trust the client has in her to hold in confidence the personal secrets divulged in the therapeutic relationship. That trust must be honored.

The Privacy Act of 1974 basically guaranteed that no written records may be kept pertaining to any individual to which that individual does not have access. The Act provides the right for:

1. The individual to review and make copies of all written records applicable to him/her.
2. The individual to request alterations to those records if they are inaccurate.
3. A legal process for individuals to use to have the records altered if informal attempts to do so are unproductive.

Concomitant regulations specified that programs that release information in violation of the new Federal Confidentiality Regulations (42 CFR Part 2) are subject to a fine of $500, for the first offense and up to $5000 for each subsequent offense. Violations of the regulations, published in the Federal Register, July 1, 1975, may be reported to the U.S. Attorney for the judicial district in which the violation occurs.

These regulations basically affect alcohol and drug abuse programs that are directly or indirectly supported or regulated by an agency of the Federal government. Thus, most treatment agencies are responsible to ensure that these regulations are adhered to by the staff. The principles and procedures for the Confidentiality and Privacy Acts must be presented to all staff and reinforced throughout the clinical supervisory relationship.

When a counselor violates these regulations, it is the legal and ethical responsibility of the clinical supervisor to intervene, mediate, and remedy the problem as soon as possible.

The same is true for the issues of professional ethics and morality. The field has been slow to develop a Code of Ethical Practice for Counselors. However, with the implementation of state and national counselor credentialling procedures, a Code has been implemented. Although all counselors operate daily within the context of a set of moral and ethical rules derived from religious, social, and family teachings, these rules are relative to the individual and subject to distortions of one's current perception of reality. A Professional Code of Ethical Practice is an attempt to limit the range of acceptable behaviors to be exhibited by counselors. The Code serves as a safeguard for the profession and the rights of the client.

(The NIAAA Code of Ethical Practice for Alcoholism Counselor Certification and the Ethical Standards of the State of Vermont Alcoholism Counselor's Association, Inc., are utilized as a guide in this context. However, to date, the NIAAA Code for Ethical Practice for Alcoholism Counselors is the most widely accepted in the field.)

A Code of Ethical Practice serves the primary function of providing a means of social control with a minimum of governmental and societal interference in the normal activities of the profession: it defines the professional conduct expected of persons in a given profession.

A Code of Ethical Practice further meets the needs of the field by:

1. safeguarding the welfare of clients
2. guarding the privacy of confidentiality regulations
3. maintaining quality service delivery within the profession
4. honestly representing the profession's qualifications
5 facilitating communication and reciprocity among all members
6 making clear distinctions between the professional's personal views and the agencies' views

It is the responsibility of the agency and the clinical supervisor to ensure that the Code of Ethical Practice is mentioned to all staff and upheld and at all times. When a person violates the Code, the supervisor must intervene quickly in the interest of the rights of the client, the responsibility of the agency, and the professionalism of the counselor himself. At times, it may be the obligation of the supervisor to aid the counselor in realizing the difficulties in the field and that he would perform better in a field of endeavor other than counseling. To perform this task, when required, is part of the supervisor's responsibility to the person himself, the program, and the public.

Certain forms of action by counselors are never permissible, such as overt or covert sexual behavior with clients, other forms of acting out, illegal actions (on or off the job), etc. Immediate attention by the supervisor to such disruptive behavior is necessary.

Does the counselor have any rights in clinical supervision? Although the primary focus of the Code of Ethical Practice is upon the rights of the client and the employing agency, the counselor is entitled to a display of respect and professional dignity by the supervisor. As specified in prior sections, the personal life of the counselor is irrelevant to the supervisor as long as it does not infringe on the clinical functioning of that person. The counselor is entitled to act, dress, and live as he desires, provided such action is consistent with the goals of the agency, and in the interest of the client.

The counselor also has the right to perform the tasks of her job without the constant vigil of the supervisor. She was hired to perform a task. She was hired with the assumption that she is a professional, and could perform those tasks. The purpose of supervision is not "snooper- vision"; it is intended to provide a resource of growth, and to ensure the delivery of the highest quality of care to clients.

On the other hand, if the counselor is in a trainee role, or if he acts clinically in a way that does not earn him that right, it is the responsibility of the supervisor to monitor and evaluate his performance more closely. Thus, semi-autonomous clinical functioning is a right of a professional, provided he has won that right based on prior training, background, and experience, and has demonstrated the ability to maintain that autonomy by acting appropriately and professionally.

Finally, the counselor has the right to deal with her patients as she prescribes and with a therapeutic approach she views appropriate, provided that behavior is consistent with the goals of the employing agency, and in the best interest of the client.

Issues in Counselor Certification

In the past five years, the substance abuse field has become obsessed, and justifiably so, with the issue of credentialling its workers. This stems from the need to assure the highest quality of care for patients, to provide a mechanism for third party reimbursement for counselors, and to provide recognition to the counselors to bring them into the mainstream of the health care delivery system. The National Institute on Alcohol Abuse and Alcoholism (NIAAA) began the effort in 1974 with the publication of the Roy Littlejohn Associates, Inc. report on counselor certification. The National Standards for Alcoholism Counselors proposed to establish a national advisory and credentialling board and standards of competencies for counselors. It was further recommended that this credentialling process be a voluntary one.

After the acceptance of the report by the NIAAA, the Institute chose not to implement the recommendations, but to abdicate the responsibility for credentialling to the states. This failure to act by the NIAAA has led to further factionalism and self-interest in the field. Credentialling has been paralyzed by haphazardly implemented processes by states by a few isolated, quasi-professional groups. Where standards were developed, the system was a patchwork of varying requirements which impeded geographic and career mobility. There was no coherent overall effort to assure a nationally recognized protocol for counselors establishing a recognized professional peerage that could be equal to other health care professional groups. Overall, the NIAAA inaction was an unwise decision in the light of the current mood in the health care delivery field.

From 1974 to 1978, a number of state alcoholism authorities and counselor associations took up the gauntlet and developed their own peer review standards and processes. By 1978, the majority of the states had developed standards for counselor credentialling; however, efforts still remained disconnected with no apparent capability for establishing interstate reciprocity. In 1976, the NIAAA established a Planning Panel under the direction of Dr. Kenneth Finger of Florida to (1) "Identify the issues relevant to credentialling of counselors; and, (2) Make recommendations to the field as to how it should proceed with the credentialling issue."

The final report of the Finger Planning Panel was delivered to the NIAAA in March of 1977, wherein the policy and procedures for establishing a national counselor credentialling mechanism was proposed (again). In 1979 this mechanism was established as the National Commission for the Credentialling of Alcoholism Counselors. The Commission may became operational in 1979 as the national, central clearinghouse for counselor certification.

It is important to examine a number of factors that relate to certification and their impact upon supervision. In those states that have implemented standards for certification, the number of hours of training required is 200–400. Many of these states have specified a minimum of 50 percent of those hours being delivered in a supervised practicum situation. The conflict is obvious: if there is little quality clinical supervision being provided, where, outside of a formal, academic training program with a field placement component can the on-line worker receive practicum experience? This points to the need to have quality clinical supervision provided on-site by the local agency.

In lieu of this capability, the Eastern Area Alcohol Education and Training Program (EAAETP) has taken the lead by establishing a Clinical Preceptorship Program, providing a network of approved clinical supervisors with outstanding clinical qualifications who can deliver the needed supervision to counselors. This is a model for supervisory training provided in other professional groups, such as, for example, the American

Association of Marriage and Family Therapists. Appendix C contains a detailed description of this training program so that counselors can meet the practicum training requirements for credentialling.

The second issue related to credentialling is the problem of evaluating counselor capabilities and competencies. The state of the art is such that objective tests of counselor skills are difficult. Subjective, clinical assessments by a skilled supervisor are essential if the credentialling bodies are to be able to validate their judgments of the counselors. Without clinical assessments, and in the absence of written tests of skills, certification groups can only make their decisions on the basis of formal criteria, such as number of years logged in the field, in training, years of sobriety, etc. These decisions cannot be made on the basis of perceived skills and competencies unless there is a system for evaluating those skills via observations by a skilled supervisor.

This again points to the importance of developing clinical supervisory skills of individuals who can provide feedback to the credentialling bodies on the qualifications of those counselors seeking certification.

DEPENDENCE VS. AUTONOMY

Supervision is at times criticized as building an interminable dependence by staff upon the supervisor. (One wishes that such a "danger" would occur in the substance abuse field given the current dearth of adequate supervision.) The issue of when to terminate supervision, however, should be addressed. At what point does a person have enough supervision? Is it a never-ending process? Would this not contribute eventually to a deterioration of the professional self-image of the counseling staff?

The principle dissatisfaction with continued supervision

seems to lie with prolonging the educational process, thus suggesting that the counselor does not know enough, is not fully competent, and is incapable of autonomous practice. One acknowledges the need to have ongoing administrative supervision but not clinical supervision.

Kadushin writes (1968)

> Even if all workers were fully trained, were objectively self-critical, and had developed a level of self-awareness that eliminated the needs for supervision, even if all were so highly motivated, so self-assured, so rich in inner resources that they felt no need for supervisory support, administrative supervision would continue to be necessary as long as the workers were employees of an agency.

Clinical supervision, however, should eventually move towards greater autonomy for the staff, with the supervisor moving out of the master-apprentice model into a comaster one. It should become an optional process sought out by the counselors when they feel the need to do so. The spirit of the clinical supervisory relationship changes accordingly. Nearly equal status is achieved so that both can communicate as peers in their clinical endeavors. This is a difficult step at which to arrive for it involves the egos of both parties. It is, however, a healthy and inevitable step for all involved if and when the transition can occur. To fail to take that step will result in interminable dependence and hostility on the part of the counselors who have achieved a level of competency to merit greater autonomy.

A team model for supervision is one means of "cutting the staff loose" from the supervisor. This model was proposed by Brieland, Briggs, and Leuenberger in 1973 and by Rowley and Faux in 1966. In this model the staff is arranged in a modified pyramidal colleagial structure with the counselors acting as a working unit with responsibility as a whole for clinical supervision of each other. The supervisor is a member of that structure, and an equal with others. She serves as a resource person to the group. Decision making must occur within the group experience with the actual supervisor validating that decision. This validation is necessary since the supervisor retains the responsibility for the functioning of that unit.

Another variation of the supervision model, proposed by Watson in 1973, is the use of a variety of supervisory procedures, such as individual tutorials, case consultations, supervisory groups, peer discussions, team supervision, etc. The combinations of approaches are healthy and productive for the agency provided the central goals of the clinical supervisory sessions are not lost. A variety of supervisory procedures adds for exploration and individualization of the process. Caution must be exerted, though, so that the authority and power for the agency performance is still vested in the program director/-administrator and/or clinical supervisor, rather than abdicated to an amorphous group process.

Chapter 8

WHAT TO SAY AFTER YOU'VE SAID HELLO

George Bernard Shaw wished that the epitaph on his gravestone read, "I knew if I stayed around long enough, something like this would happen." Many clinical supervisors adopt this attitude by hoping that key issues will eventually emerge in supervisory sessions without structuring or directing the sessions in the desired direction. This chapter is written to assist the supervisor in getting beyond simply saying hello in sessions.

Clinical supervision is an intensive tutorial process, involving an exploration of personal and clinical issues. Many alcoholism and drug abuse clinical supervisors confuse periodic discussions about cases with the active, intensive learning experience of supervision. It means more than learning 150 ways to say "ah-ha." It means an ongoing dialogue between a counseling "master" and "apprentice."

To stimulate the supervisor to explore the full range of issues, this chapter will outline the various phases of the clinical supervisory process; the "topics" for discussion in supervision, such as transference, and countertransference, sexual conflicts, manifest and latent content in counseling sessions, etc.; and tendencies of entry-level counselors. The chapter will conclude with an illustration of a specific therapeutic technique (gestalt therapy) as utilized in a clinical supervisory session experienced by the author as a trainee.

PHASES OF SUPERVISION

Clinical supervision, as any learning process, moves through a series of phases that determine the scope, intensity, and subject matter for discussion. These phases occur primarily when working with entry-level counselors with a limited degree of clinical or academic experience.

Phase One: "In the Beginning"

The initial phase of clinical supervision is "diagnostic" in nature in that it addresses issues such as establishing position, time, space, recordkeeping for the sessions, and the selection of cases geared to the skills, personality, and learning needs of the counselors.

Research has demonstrated that supervisee needs and interest in supervision change over time. In the initial phase of supervision, beginning counselors benefit more when the sessions focus on procedural and administrative issues of counseling. The clarification of issues such as clinical dynamics, transference, catharsis, etc., are issues which tend to appear more often in the second and third phases of clinical supervision. Thus, there should be a developmental sequence to the evolution of supervisee's needs over the course of the supervision.

In the initial phase, there is a danger of the supervisor overpsychologizing the situation in hopes of rapidly inculcating the counselors with therapeutic skills before they are ready and able to learn this material. From the beginning, the supervisor should help the trainees to take responsibility for their own learning and problem-solving process, rather than telling or showing them the way.

Another initial trap for the supervisor is to dominate the process in hopes of establishing his own credibility. The saying is "He who can, supervises; he who cannot, advertises his methods." A clinical supervisor is well advised to establish his credibility by role modeling, by being viewed in action rather than in words, by propagandizing and proselytizing. Although novice supervisors sense a pressure to be viewed as an experienced counselor, one's anxiety must be tempered realizing that the counselor in the beginning is probably as anxious, if not more so, than the supervisor.

The developmental tasks to be dealt with in the first phase of clinical supervision are as follows:

1. Counselors need to learn how to listen to patients. Beginning counselors seem to need to develop the ability to hear what the client is saying, and attend to various levels of communication (latent and manifest). Novice counselors tend to take content at face value without listening to the covert messages, verbal and nonverbal cues, etc.
2. The supervisor needs to help the counselors to develop a sense of passive receptivity to this communication by increasing their propensity to listen and inhibit the urge to respond. Advice giving and story telling are common responses, especially for the novice counselor.
3. In the beginning phase, supervisees value the supervisor when she attends to detail, carefully listening to the data presented by the counselor and client. The supervisor's attentive attitude is a role model for the counselors on therapeutic attending. The supervisor is thus teaching the staff how to attend to the immediate situation.

4. In phase one of supervision, counselors tend to distrust the supervisor who engages in speculative thinking. Beginners prefer complete explanations of the supervisor's chain of reasoning. How did you get to that conclusion? This can be a painstaking, plodding, but inevitable process for the supervisor because excessive abstract theorizing by the supervisor in the beginning will not be helpful.
5. Entry-level counselors want advice and suggestions of a technical and procedural nature from the supervisor. "What should I do? How do I handle this situation?" Cookbook answers are sought. They tend to resent passivity and nondirectiveness by the supervisor, feeling that he is deliberately withholding useful information from them. If the supervisor does not fall into this trap, they learn not to expect this from the supervisor and begin to problem-solve for themselves.
6. In the beginning, counselors tend to be defensive of criticism which is viewed as being painful and damaging. It is difficult for the counselors to use constructive criticism, constructively. Group criticism is limited and appears like "two fighters hitting each other with cream puffs." Since the counselors are initially seeking confidence building, the supervisor should seek to establish a healthy atmosphere for learning by building on strengths and not weaknesses, and helping counselors to feel better about themselves and their abilities.

When supervision is conducted in a small group setting, there are a number of tasks through which the group moves. These tasks are not sequential, and are similar to the tasks of most groups (treatment, educational, remedial, etc.). Once a supervisor understands the concepts of the developmental group tasks (which parallel the tasks or phases outlined above) he will be more able to maintain objectivity in supervision.

In the first phase of group clinical supervision, sessions are characterized by:

Limit setting on honesty, confidentiality, sexuality issues, etc.

"In/out" issues. Generally the course of events in early group clinical supervision meetings is influenced by the group members with the "loudest" problem (not necessarily the most severe or neediest, but the most immediately manifest). Usually, however, this group provocateur drops out of the process early. The supervisor must recognize this person and clarify his role in the group to help prevent the person from committing social suicide.

A lack of risk-taking, feeling each other out instead.

Superficiality, circumstantiality, restricted and stereotyped conversation.

Denial, resistance to self-examination and disclosure.

Pairing.

Rationality, promoting group tranquility.

It is the basic task of the supervisor and the group to do the following:

Determine a method of achieving the primary group goals ("a search for meaning").

Attend to social relationships, role setting, who will be respected, ignored, rejected, accepted, liked, etc.

Answer issues of how much to be revealed.

Address dependency issues and needs. Early group clinical supervisory sessions look to the supervisor to provide answers and acceptance. The supervisor owes them answers, they think. He should be aware of his own anxieties to "produce magic" in his desire to get things going. Patience, in this case, is a virtue.

Practice "goblet therapy" where there is an attempt to have endless discussions of matters of little substance, and to engage in never-ending exploratory forays.

Whether clinical supervision is provided in either a group or individual context, the supervisor must be aware of the dynamics of this first phase so she will be able to work through the various tasks in a constructive manner.

Phase Two: "The Middle Period"

Trainees in this phase have a greater desire to discuss theories than in phase one. They wish to expand the boundaries of their experiences, to generalize from the specific to the general, and to integrate experience and knowledge into a coherent theoretical framework. Counselors begin to identify with a particular school of thought.

At this phase, the more advanced the trainee the more receptive she will be to criticism. She will display the self-confidence to face critical feedback. The supervisor's brilliant deductive leaps will be more stimulating to the counselors at this phase of the process. What might be unsettling to the novice counselor is, at this point, interesting and exciting.

In group clinical supervision, after the initial phase, the focus changes form "in/out" to "top/bottom" matters. Preoccupations with approval, acceptance, etc. moves to a preoccupation with dominance, control, and power. The conflict is often between the counselors and the supervisor, with each supervisee attempting to establish his own amount of power, social pecking order, and dominance in the group and in general.

Second phase groups are characterized by hostile comments and intermember criticism, judgments of others, and one-way analyses. Advice-giving with abandoned social conventions begins. "Oughts" and "shoulds" are heard. A "peer court" is established. There is a jockeying for position and a hostility and ambivaleance towards the supervisor. The sources of negativism are obviously due to the unrealistic magical attitudes with which many counselors secretly imbue the supervisor. They are unconsciously disappointed by her limitations. Also, each counselor in phase one has been seeking to be the favored one; they know now that no one is favored. The rivalous feelings towards each other are turned upon the supervisor.

Lest the supervisor panic at this phase, it should be remembered that the counselors are usually not unanimous in their attacks. A champion for the supervisor usually emerges. Patience again is key.

Possible efforts to unseat the supervisor may occur, to hold a leaderless group, to begin the sessions before the supervisor arrives. He should beware lest he transmit covert signals of personal distress and threat by these actions. Finally, the degree of hostility is dependent on his style of supervision and behavior.

This phase of supervision is often difficult and unpleasant for the supervisor, although it is essential to group survival and the learning process. The supervisor should discriminate between attacks on her personally, and her role as an authority figure.

If the supervisor cannot deal with the hostility in this phase of supervision, it will result in displaying a desire to be loved; remaining aloof, or displaying ambiguity or profundity; displaced off-target attacks from the group; group taboos that are counter-honesty and counter-productive to learning; a loss of the group's model setting potential; scapegoating by the group.

Again, an understanding by the supervisor of these phases will assist him in enhancing the learning process and acting in a positive, constructive manner.

Phase Three: "The Final Period"

Counselors at this phase of their development sincerely desire to learn about their own functioning. They are more relaxed as counselors and wish to examine their role, feelings, countertransferences, reactions, conscious and unconscious material, impasses in personal and professional behavior, etc. For this to happen a trust level must have been established between counselor and supervisor. This phase of group clinical supervision focuses on "near/far" issues, intimacy and closeness. Very few group clinical supervisory sessions reach this phase of development.

Although these groups offer greater freedom of self-disclosure, there may also be other communicational restrictions, such as suppression of all negative expressions in the service of group cohesion, ("sweetness and light" issues). The clinical supervisory group basks in its glow of its newly discovered unity. Eventually, though, the glow pales and permits hostility again and thus becomes an ongoing work-study group.

Tasks that are apparent in this phase of supervision are in-group cohesiveness ("we-consciousness"); common goals, group spirit; consensus action; cooperation, mutual support, and integration; freedom of communication, self-disclosure; increased morale, mutual trust; sexual secrets revealed; countertransferences presented; long-buried transgressions unearthed; postgroup meetings; and attendance improvements and concern shown for missing group members. In sum, each group clinical supervisory session works through various tasks, so much so that the supervisor can estimate the age of the group by the tasks through which the counselors are working.

Throughout these phases, the supervisor focuses on a number of items "after he has said hello." The exploratory process is aided by the clinical supervisor asking relevant questions, requesting information, adding to the counselors' thinking, calling attention to the clients' and counselors' behaviors, focusing on missed opportunities, significant interactions, misinterpretations, gaps, inconsistencies, and parapraxes in the clinical event.

Although this book is not intended to be a text on psychopathology, a few brief definitions are necessary, especially for the clinical supervisor with limited background and exposure to these terms.

PARAPRAXES Parapraxes are euphemistically called "Freudian slips," that reinforce the old proverb that "a slip of the tongue betrays the true state of mind." In psychoanalytic theory, the emergence of an otherwise unconscious tendency is due to the temporary inability of the ego to control it or to integrate it in normal fashion with the other psychic tendencies which are active within the mind at the same time.

However, whether one accepts the Freudian explanation for parapraxes, it has long been accepted that if, for example, Mr. Smith forgets Miss Jones' name or called her Miss Robinson "by mistake" Miss Jones would ordinarily react to it as an intentional slight or sign of disinterest. "Slips" are taken in both common parlance and in psychological theory seriously and are viewed as the result of a purposeful action of the individual involved, although the intent may be unknown to the person himself.

"Slips" occur often in counseling sessions, and may be missed by an involved counselor. This "material" should be pointed out to the counselor as relevant to the therapeutic process.

The supervisor can indicate counselor rigidity and lack of security about himself. The counselor's attitude about the client can be questioned. New concepts and ideas about counseling can be introduced by the supervisor. Current research and knowledge in the field can be shared. Analogies to the clinical material can be made. Thus, the viewpoint of the counselor can be expanded in the clinical supervisory sessions.

The supervisor further aids in clarifying the goals for the particular client and in conceptualizing the client–counselor relationship. Counselors should be able to identify their own feelings and attitudes about the client.

CATHARSIS Catharsis is an important process in the supervisory sessions as well as discussions of transference and countertransference in the clinical relationship. Catharsis is the outpouring of pent-up emotions in a cleansing process. It is often the first and necessary step towards a reorientation of the person in treatment. As a client experiences the free expression of emotions, catharsis occurs. At times, counselors miss opportunities for encouraging catharsis, either because of blindness during the clinical event to the emotional process underway, or because of a desire to avoid the level of emotionality which overflows in the cathartic process. The supervisor can aid the counselor in pointing out missed opportunities or unobserved outpourings by the client.

TRANSFERENCE Transference is based on the premise that any relationship is social and involves an emotional response. This is especially true in the counseling relationship where the client experiences and expresses feelings towards the counselor that he felt towards figures important in his life: mother, father, siblings, husband, wife, lover, etc. Novice counselors tend to miss the nuances of the relationship and are unaware of these dynamics in the counseling relationship. The supervisor should point out transference reactions by the client.

An example of transference is provided from the author's practice with a young female client who entered each session angry after having to wait two or three minutes for the session to begin. After five minutes waiting she was tearful and hostile. She fantasized that I was providing extra time to another female client. After a number of sessions and the establishment of a trusting relationship, she was able to recall her reactions as a little girl of five when her father kept her waiting to come to her room for a goodnight hug and kiss. He would always go to kiss the older, "favorite" daughter first. Her tearful, jealous response to me was a fantasizing of these early childhood memories. The key to understanding the office behavior was in recognizing the repetitive past experiences, or transference reactions.

Another example of transference is of a client the author treated for two years. As a spouse of an alcoholic, she experienced physical and emotional pain. She expected a similar reaction in the clinical relationship: ambiguity, rejection, hostility, and parental condemnations. After considerable effort, she was able to recall her punitive family environment as a child and her violent and hostile father. She fantasized that if she was able to anger me, she would again be able to have a "father" relationship with another male, even as she had done with her husband and "lovers." The fantasies of early childhood and the repetitions of past object relationships were being played out for her in the counseling relationship as well.

With this specific case, there were a number of other transference reactions played out in the counseling sessions, the most dramatic of which was her memories at the age of 10 when she was raped by her brother. For a time, she perceived me as that brother who was threatening her sexuality. The realization of this relationship brought about a flood of emotions and helped in the resolution of those earlier memories.

In both cases, it was essential that the counselor be aware of the transference reactions lest they interfere in the therapeutic process. In the latter case, the insight and knowledge of a clinical supervisor was necessary to bring these matters to my awareness.

COUNTERTRANSFERENCE Countertransference is a reciprocal response by a counselor to a client. These are harder to get at since the counselor often is unaware of his reactions. These responses are almost certain to interfere with the counselor's therapeutic effectiveness. They are a result of the patient's influence on the counselor's feelings and are based on the latter's irrational projections and identifications. The counselor must not permit his own feelings and attitudes to intrude in the clinical relationship. The supervisor can aid the counselor in realizing his reactions and in the resolution process.

The author recalls one of his first clients while working in a state mental hospital. The patient was severely disturbed, with delusions, hallucinations, and paranoid behavior. He would frequently hit his head against the wall to the point that blood flowed. After the first few sessions, I was irritable and had nightmares about this client killing himself. His face kept appearing in my sleep. It was not until a wise clinical supervisor assisted in realizing the physical resemblance to my own father and the trauma I felt upon the sight of blood on the patient's head that I was able to resolve the countertransference reactions. At that point, the therapeutic relationship improved significantly.

In these cases the clinical supervisor acts as a mirror on the counselor–client relationship. Irrelevant inferences and projections by the counselor are pointed out. "How do you feel about this client?" is a question that can frequently be asked of the supervisee. The manifest and latent content of the clinical event is thus explored by the supervisor and counselor.

MANIFEST CONTENT Manifest content is the remembered aspects of the material discussed. Manifest impulses often combine materials from immediate experiences with emotions and thoughts of the past. This occurs through condensation, displacement, and symbolization. Latent content is the meaning of material that is not directly expressed by the client. A gifted clinical supervisor will alert the counselor to both levels of communication that occur in the counseling event and in the supervisory relationship.

In the initial clinical supervisory sessions, the focus of the discussion may be upon the dimensions of a nourishing therapeutic relationship, such as the four basic Carkhuff dimensions or characteristics of effective counselor behavior:

1. Empathetic understanding. The counselors' effectiveness is directly related to one's increase in the depth of understanding. Self-understanding translates directly to one's ability to be aware of what the client is saying.
2. Respect. This is positive regard, or nonpossessive warmth which begins in the respect which the counselor has for herself. The counselor cannot respect the problems and background of clients if she cannot respect her own feelings and experiences.
3. Genuineness. The counselor must be honest with himself and with the client. The basis for the entire therapeutic process is found in the genuine relationship between counselor and patient.
4. Personally-relevant concreteness. The counselor must be able to directly express feelings and experiences, regardless of their emotional content. The only qualification is that the "material" must be of personally meaningful relevance to the client.

For a further explanation of the Carkhuff model for counselor skills, especially as applied to substance abuse counselors, the reader is referred to the book by Stephen Valle, *Alcoholism Counselors: The Emergence of a New Profession.*

To return to the subject of "what to say after you've said hello," the supervisory relationship itself can, at times, become an example of how the counselor is relating to clients. Interactions between the supervisor and supervisee can become the live material for discussion.

The sessions can focus on issues such as non-verbal behaviors of client and counselor. Non-verbal behaviors are addressed in three areas, all of which can be dealt with by a skilled supervisor:

Proxemics—The study of the spatial arrangement and its effect on interaction. This may be termed "body space."

Kinesics—Communications through gestures, posture, facial expressions, and body movement.

Paralanguage—The non-verbal aspects of vocalization.

Other areas not yet greatly explored are tactile, and artifactual. Non-verbal communications serve as safety valves to express emotions which cannot be safely expressed verbally, such as sticking one's tongue out. The ways in which these emotional tones are expressed vary greatly between cultures. Proper interpretation by a counselor requires familiarity with the sender's culture and background. When one is skilled at interpreting non-verbal communication, he is often also gifted at interpreting emotional undertones. The supervisor can translate such nonverbal behaviors (both of the counselor and the client) in the clinical supervisory sessions.

Supervisory sessions can also focus on significant transitions, eye contact, and client thought processes, such as denials and perseverations, etc. Perseverations are the persistent recurrence of a single association in which the client seems to be incapable of shifting from the idea once it has been expressed. This clinging to a thought may be observed at times in aphasis, alcoholic stupor, hallucinations, etc. In the "heat" of the counseling event, the counselor may not "hear" these recurrent themes and thus miss what is being told to him about the emotional and intellectual functioning of the client. It is the supervisor's responsibility to point out unobserved processes.

Sessions can also focus on other conscious and unconscious material: tardiness by both the counselor and the client; the use of humor and other anxiety indicators; speech patterns; game-playing by both parties; overt and covert sexual issues; counseling approaches; keys to motivating the client to change; case termination procedures; and differential diagnostic techniques.

Differential diagnosis is a process often avoided by alcoholism and drug abuse counselors because of the philosophical premise that alcoholic clients' basic problem is alcohol. Personality disorders will diminish and disappear when the alcohol is removed from the system. This leads to an oversimplification of the diagnostic process and reductionism. Significant pathology is missed until the client acts out in a destructive manner, at which point it may be too late.

The author recalls a number of clients in an alcoholism treatment program in New Jersey who had given definite signs of suicidal ideation. But, the alcoholism counselors were not looking for other pathologies besides the drinking behavior. Two suicide attempts were necessary before the staff began to be more aware of psychopathologic signs of clients.

The clinical supervisor should assist staff in understanding the constitutional, neurological, physiological, social, and psychogenic factors that the life history of the client reveals that are useful in developing a diagnosis, prognosis, and treatment plan. The alcoholism counselor can be alerted by a skilled supervisor to these various dimensions of the clients's history. "Mini" courses in psychopathology and differential diagnosis are useful, especially for the nondegreed counselor who has had limited to no background in psychopathology.

These issues provide challenging material for exploration between supervisor and supervisee. Far too few counselors in the substance abuse field are aware and able to deal with these matters because of a lack of training in psychotherapeutic skills. Counseling is viewed by many as using AA Twelve-Step counseling methods in a clinical setting. However, to avoid these issues in supervisory sessions is to display one's ignorance of the complexities of the counseling process, and to do a disservice to the staff and to the client.

Research in the EAAETP Clinical Preceptorship Program (see Appendix C) has indicated a number of areas of skill building that clinical supervisors should focus on in the training of counselors. Overall, counselors in the field appear to have adequate interpersonal abilities, being capable of getting along well with co-workers. Staff morale generally is acceptable, with highly motivated, dedicated counselors. There is a profound sense of empathy, and caring about the concerns of the client.

Counselors seem to have a good sense of their limits with healthy attitudes about their functioning.

Probably the greatest asset that the alcoholism counselor brings to his work is his affective qualities: empathy, respect, genuineness, concreteness, and congruence. However, when all else fails, and when they are uncertain about what to do in a counseling session, they utilize their own life experiences and not always skillfully. A sense of timing and appropriateness of self-disclosure needs to be cultivated with the assistance of the clinical supervisor.

Alcoholism counselors also need to develop a sense of self-esteem as professionals. An awareness of their own competency and professionalism needs to grow. Although they suspect they are good counselors, they need to hear over a period of time that they are. This is the responsibility of the clinical supervisor to provide this positive reinforcement.

Nondegreed alcoholism counselors need to be able to better develop treatment goals and be able to relate these to the clients. Assistance is needed by the supervisor in conceptualizing the goals for treatment. Simplistic goal-setting occurs wherein all clients are "squeezed into" one treatment model, not allowing for individual client differences.

Further skill development training is needed in applying appropriate therapeutic techniques in particular clinical situations, and in identifying personality disorders. These are "blind spots" in the differential diagnostic processes of the counselors. The tendency is to broadly categorize all clients, without particular attention to individualizing the diagnostic procedures.

Some counselors need basic training in listening and processing. Counselors in the field have a tendency to "tell the client what is wrong with him," making the patient an audience for a "therapeutic show."

Supervisors also need to focus on "family thinking." There is a tendency for counselors to refer any problems with "family overtones" to another worker, whether or not that problem should more appropriately be dealt with by the primary counselor assigned to the case. There is a lack of awareness by counselors of family systems and dynamics and supervisors should assist them in this "gap" in their clinical functioning.

Clinical supervisors should also aid counselors in involving the client in his own treatment processes via a problem-solving methodology. The client's innate abilities need to be mobilized. There is a tendency among alcoholism counselors to describe the client's problems for them, rather than allowing the client to arrive at his own solutions.

Also, nondegreed counselors function at a "gut" level, using intuitive sense. Supervisors should assist counselors in understanding and verbalizing what they are doing, and why. What are the responses of the client that triggered those clinical responses? This involves, for some counselors, resolving the conflict over reacting professionally vs. spontaneously, and intuitively. It involves aiding the staff to identify their own assumptive systems.

In addition to these issues to be focused on by the supervisor, counselors need assistance in overcoming basic roadblocks to communication, which are so characteristic of entry-level helping agents. There is a tendency of counselors to order, direct, admonish, and command clients by telling them what to do. The client's feelings and needs are unimportant; he must comply with the counselor's feelings. This is especially true for the evangelistic approaches of Twelve-Step counseling. Anger and resentment, however, grows in the client since the counselor does not really trust the client's problem-solving abilities.

The messages conveyed by the counselor are "You should do it the way I did when I was recovering." "You will be sorry if you do that." "Don't talk to your children like that." "Stop complaining. Do as I do." These messages make the client feel fearful, angry, resentful, and hostile.

A related counselor response is overanalysis and interpretation of the client's behaviors: "You don't believe that at all, now do you?" If the analysis is accurate, the client feels embarassed; if it is not, he feels angry and misjudged. Supervisors should point out to the counselor when he is ordering, directing, admonishing, or commanding clients.

Novice counselors tend to preach and exhort the client to behave in a particular way, with "shoulds" and "oughts" as the basis of their communication. "Don't trust yourself" is the message. "When I was drinking. . . ." "Take my advice. . . ." "The solution to your problem is. . . ." "Just wait a few months before you do that. I did."

Giving advice sometimes results in the client devoting his attention to the counselor's ideas to the exclusion of developing his own ideas. Yet, when all else fails for the new counselor, packaged solutions, advice-giving based on his own life experiences, lecturing, logically arguing the client out of his behavior, etc., seems to be the only resource when one is not certain how to deal with the client.

Judging, shaming, criticizing, ridiculing, disagreeing, name-calling, and blaming behavior is at times displayed by counselors. Supervisors should point out this behavior when it is apparent. The messages are "You are not thinking clearly." "That is an immature action." "You are inferior, unworthy, because of your response." "Drinking like that is stupid." "Don't you know you are killing yourself." "You should feel foolish, shamed." "You are nothing but a lush."

The client hears messages of his inadequacy and destroys an already weak self-image. He feels stupid, shamed, and unloved by his counselor. Defensive feelings are invoked to protect his self-image. Often the client will become angry and feel hatred towards the counselor, even if the judgment is accurate. This behavior by the counselor must be recognized by the supervisor.

Inappropriate reassuring, humoring, consoling, and supporting the client can be a defensive gesture by a counselor who is "looking for success" by pointing to the positive, even in the face of problems. The message conveyed is that the counselor does not really understand the client's pain or that he is uncomfortable with that hurt. The client hears that he should stop feeling that way.

These responses are also perceived as diverting attention from substantive issues, withdrawing from self, and pushing the problem aside. The counselor communicates a lack of interest in the client's feelings. The messages are "Let's talk about that in upcoming sessions." "You will feel better tomorrow." "I used to think that way also, but now I'm better." "We have been through all that before." "You have the ability to do well so let's not deal with that."

Such positive evaluations do not fit the self-image of the client, who feels manipulated by being told what he wants to hear. Counselors have a tendency to respond this way in hopes of providing reassurance in times of crisis. From a therapeutic point of view, however, it is counterproductive and should be dealt with by the clinical supervisor.

Finally, novice counselors can adopt a questioning, probing, and interrogating stance towards the client, trying to find the reasons, motives, and causes for the behavior. Such questions convey a lack of trust. Questions are raised as to the freedom of the person to talk about whatever he wants to. Although questioning and probing is necessary to get adequate information to proceed, when used as a basic counseling style throughout the sessions, it communicates messages of distance. The words used are "What put that idea in your head?" "Why do you feel that way? You shouldn't!" "Tell me about your childhood. Every last detail."

These responses are found periodically in initial counseling styles. Attention must be paid by the clinical supervisor to confront the counselor when these roadblocks to therapeutic communication are observed. Modeling by the clinical supervisor of positive communication patterns further enhances this process of observation and change.

The above are a number of topics and skills which can be addressed in clinical supervisory sessions. It must always be remembered, however, that the "curriculum" for sessions develops out of the specific training needs of each counselor. The above suggestions are presented merely as stimulators and indicators of needs that have been identified for some counselors.

What does a clinical supervisor say after he has said hello? In summary he focuses on the full range of personal and professional counseling issues as they apply to the clinical functioning of the staff. Gaps in the knowledge of the counselors should be filled by the supervisor. Skill building occurs as the minutest detail of clinical functioning is explored and analyzed.

In concluding this chapter, a detailed clinical supervisory session from the author's experience will be presented to illustrate the range of issues that can be addressed and the techniques which can be employed by a clinical supervisor. The following is a condensed version of an actual clinical supervisory session.

Mrs. Smith, a client under my care, came for treatment with the presenting problem of sleeplessness and general anxiety. After some discussion it was revealed that she was engaged in a number of extramarital affairs, each involving extensive systems of deception and lying to her spouse. The relationships involved a variety of "imaginative and creative" sexual experiences from sodomy, incest, and group sex. As the therapist, I felt we were at an impasse in the treatment process. We seemed to be going nowhere and I was experiencing concern and discomfort over the lack of progress in counseling.

This case was presented in a series of individual clinical supervisory sessions. In one session, the clinical supervisor (C.S.), gifted in gestalt therapy techniques, sought to assist in overcoming my barriers with the case. The supervisor did not help solve the problem but helped reestablish the conditions under which I (D.P.) could best use my own problem-solving abilities.

Being aware of "splits" in my attention and awareness, the clinical supervisor inquired into what I was doing with my legs and body. The following dialogue transpired:

C.S. Are you aware of what your body is doing?
D.P. No, not really.
C.S. What are you doing with your legs?
D.P. (Slightly startled) My legs are crossed?
C.S. Can you describe what you are doing?
D.P. I am leaning on my right thigh, resting my body on the right hand side.
C.S. On your right side?
D.P. Yes, I am resting on my right thigh, with my left side slightly off the chair. The weight of my body is on the right side, leaning away from the left.
C.S. What do you feel in your right thigh?
D.P. It is stable, solid, and comfortable.
C.S. What do you feel in your left thigh?
D.P. It is uncomfortable, trembling a bit, unsolid, not resting on anything at all.
C.S. Can you be your right side now? Write a dialogue for it!
D.P. I am David's right thigh. I find it steady, solid, leaning away from the other side, the left. . . . I keep pulling away to the solid side. I feel right, comfortable, secure, on the right basis, grounded, warm, stable.
C.S. Sounds like you are "on the right side."
D.P. Yes, it feels good, "right" if you will.
C.S. Can you be your left side now?
D.P. I am David's left side. I feel disconnected, unstable, just not comfortable or secure. I feel wrong. Not right. I am hanging suspended in the air. Unrelated and turned away from the right side.
C.S. What do you feel?
D.P. I feel wrong, like I have done something wrong. Sinned. Like something is unacceptable to the right side.
C.S. Does that remind you of anything?
D.P. Only the Bible passage about being on the right hand side of God. In the Bible they speak of those that are accepted by God, those on His right side. They were in God's will, as being accepted. Boy, this is taking me back to my old

Sunday school days. Those on the left side were cast out for their sins. They were wrong and rejected by God. Those on the right were accepted.

C.S. And here is a way of looking at what is happening. In your therapeutic impasse, you are leaning away from the left side, from the wrong, what the Bible condemns as sinful behavior. You have judged something as being against God's will and thus are leaning away from it.

D.P. Yes, I see.

C.S. Pointing this out, though, has no real effect until you take ownership for it, and relate it to Ms. Smith. Do you view Ms. Smith's behavior as wrong?

D.P. Yes, I guess I do. She is being promiscious in being unaccepted by society for her actions. I think she is wrong in the sexual acting out; it is inappropriate behavior.

C.S. You have judged her as being wrong and therefore have difficulty working through that relationship. You are at an impasse with her because of your judgments.

This realization was the beginning of a new relationship with Ms. Smith and insight into the countertransference responses to the client. The impasse was overcome and therapeutic growth began again.

This is an example of the use of a specific counseling technique in clinical supervision to bring about a change in the counselor's personal and professional development. It is something that can be said "after you have said hello."

Chapter 9

CASE MANAGEMENT PROCEDURES

A Model for Client Tracking

Although the primary focus of this text is upon techniques of clinical supervision, an integral part of the supervisor's job is administrative, involving the maintanance of an effective system for case management. The supervisor is responsible for setting general organizational policies and objectives, establishing specific tasks and duties for staff to fulfill these goals, and assigning work responsibilities and tasks to staff. She is responsible for maintaining a constant, constructive flow of work, ensuring continuity of client care and the delivery of the highest degree of clinical services.

The assignment of tasks is key to the clinical supervisor's job. Variables that will determine case assignments are:

strengths and weaknesses of counselors
complexity of casework demands

likelihood of success of counselors with various types of clients

job pressures, such as scheduling issues, staff availability, current caseloads, work flow, etc.

diversity of cases being handled by counselors and the variety of work assignments

age, sex, ethnicity of worker, and clientele

counselor's knowledge of case characteristics and/or familiarity with the individual

counselor's case preferences

Related to the clinical supervisor's task of case assignment is the responsibility of case review—knowing the progress of the counselors' caseloads. These are the case management functions of the supervisor. Coordination of unit functions, ensuring continuity of care and client flow throughout the system are the specific issues related to case review.

To reiterate from Chapter 3, the goal of case management is to gather and share information about the agency's function and client flow to ensure the effective administration of the program. It generally occurs by unit and with agency-wide personnel in interdisciplinary case reviews. The focus of the sessions is on continuity of care and case planning.

For the clinical supervisor to perform these duties, it is essential that the agency develop a coordinated system for data collection, tracking, and case management. Thorough communication between all elements of service facilitating patient flow throughout the agency must be established lest the clients "slip through the seams."

Alcoholism and Mental Health Programs at Two Agencies

The following is a model for case management developed by the Alcoholism and Mental Health Programs of the Perth

Amboy General Hospital and the Raritan Bay Community Mental Health Center in New Jersey.

In many treatment agencies there are multiple points of entry into the system. Intake and patient record system procedures must reflect this diversity. The points of entry into the Perth Amboy system were:

Emergency room
Inpatient Unit
Outpatient Unit (on a scheduled basis)
Day Hospital
Walk-in to Outpatient Clinic
Telephone contact (crisis intervention counseling)
Employees Assistance Program
Drug Abuse Unit
Adolescent Unit

To coordinate the client admissions process, the clinical supervisor assumed responsibility to facilitate client flow and functioned as the liaison between all elements of service. The clinical supervisor was lodged at the outpatient unit and was responsible for the case management procedures for the alcoholism program in all elements of service. The supervisor was kept informed daily of all admissions into the various units.

Upon admission, the case was assigned by the supervisor to a counselor for intake and completion of the necessary evils: data collection forms. The intake interview was conducted to determine the nature of the presenting problem and the patient's short/long-term treatment goals. Waiting lists for care were considered to be antithetical to the concept of the delivery of effective service. Intakes were conducted by the assigned counselor at the point of entry.

In the Perth Amboy General Hospital system, the case was

discussed at a weekly disposition conference. Patients entering through the emergency room or inpatient units were presented at both daily intake rounds, conducted by the clinical supervisor, medical doctor, and unit staff, and at the weekly disposition conference.

The purpose of the daily intake rounds and weekly disposition conference was to provide an administrative and clinical procedure for the evaluation and disposition of all cases. Further, these meetings provided an opportunity for the staff to be aware of patients in the system, to avoid duplication of services, and to facilitate client flow between units. The final assignment of the primary counselor, treatment planning, and diagnosis was completed at the disposition meetings. Staff members from all units of service attended the conferences.

To many clinical supervisors, these conferences represent what they term "clinical supervision." They mistake a management procedure for a clinical, training process. This distinction, if it has not as yet been clarified, must be indelibly imprinted in our minds.

The Perth Amboy Programs case management system included a number of additional components such as the predischarge treatment planning for all inpatients, including weekly visits to the outpatient unit by the client prior to discharge. AA meetings were held at the outpatient facility, and attended by inpatients, thus also enhancing the flow process for the client between units. Whenever possible, the client was followed upon discharge from the inpatient unit by the local visiting nurse association. This provided the agency with a clearer picture of the living arrangements and medical needs of the client. A uniform client filing system existed for all elements of service. This served to standardize the information recorded on clients throughout their care, facilitating client information flow, and enhancing intra-agency communication. An individual case file was kept on all clients that included all standardized forms, counselor progress notes, diagnostic information, medical records, psychological profiles, etc. This file followed the client throughout the treatment system, in whatever element of service care was provided. This method is far superior to a multifile system for each unit of service. The key to this procedure, however, is to have an efficient supervisor (and clerical support) which can deliver the case file to the unit of service immediately upon entrance. A comprehensive client tracking system was also used. The Alcoholism Treatment Program of Perth Amboy General Hospital utilized the following tracking system:

1st week after last visit: An initial telephone call to determine client's interest in further treatment

2nd week after last visit: Repeat telephone call

3rd week after last visit: Form letter sent

4th week after last visit: Second letter, and telephone call

5th week after last visit: Home visit, if indicated

6th week after last visit: Telephone call. If no result, case is terminated. A closing statement is provided by the primary counselor, appropriate forms completed, file retagged and case closed.

The Alcoholism Treatment Program of Perth Amboy General Hospital maintained a staff member specifically for the task of client tracking. However, such a procedure should be maintained by the clinical staff, with the clinical supervisor overseeing the process, in the absence of a "tracker."

The coordinating element in the Perth Amboy case management system was the central card file on all clients. This served to assign case numbers, provide a constant source of information on client location and status, and ensure the administrative facilitation of client transfers between units. The file was arranged as follows: two (2) distinct sets of 3 X 5 file card sections (open and closed cases) in alphabetical order, and color tagged to coordinate with the designated element of service color. A log was kept to assign case numbers for all elements of care.

Another key element in an effective case management system is the development and refinement of a standardized method for case presentations. Unfortunately, most counselors do not know how to discuss cases at staff conferences. The data presented ends up being anecdotal and disconnected. To standardize the case presentation process, the following format might be utilized: (This format is designed for an alcoholism treatment agency but can be adopted to any treatment system and clientele)

SUGGESTED OUTLINE FOR CASE PRESENTATIONS

Client name:
Town or residence:
Age:
Marital status (number of marriages, number and ages of children):
Occupation or trade:
Employment status:
Referral source:
Presenting complaints: (verbatim and counselor's impression):
Diagnosis:
History of present problem:

Years drinking
Longest period of sobriety
Recent drinking patterns
Medical complications, history
Hospitalizations, number, length of time, dates
Arrests, charges, time spent in jail
Suicical or homicidal ideation, gestures
Job or situational changes
Previous treatment

Interview results:

I. Behavior and appearance

Preliminary attitudes
Entry into room
Brief physical description, cleanliness, clothing (typical/-atypical, bizarre, unusual)
Unusual physical characteristics
Attire, build
Quality of rapport
Orality, withdrawing, manipulative, seductive
Posture (tension, rigidity, appropriateness)
Facial expressions
Cooperativeness, domineering, provocative, suspicious, overly compliant, hyperactive, depressiveness
Lethargy, distractability, shyness, dependency
Anxiety, hostility, friendliness, fears, apprehensions,
Mannerisms, suggestive verbalizations
Handedness
Recurring themes
General body movements (accelerated, decreased, inappropriateness, fidgity, restlessness)
Amplitude and quality of speech (slurring, stammering, loud, soft)

II. Affect

Appropriateness, flat, absence of affect
Depressed, anxious, happy, anger, bizarreness
Mood differences of changes (euphoria, elation, apprehension)
Blandness, lability of affect

III. Intellectual functioning

Efficiency, mental deficiency, abstraction ability and calculation ability

Reality testing, disorientation to person, place, and time
Thought disordering (obsessions, compulsions, phobias, depersonalizations, derealization, suicidal or homicial ideation)
Clarity, goal directedness, insight ability, blaming
Appropriateness, coherence
Attention, concentration, breaks, impaired level of consciousness
Discrepancy, preseverations, delusions, ideas of influence/reference
Process tendencies (associational disturbances)
Perceptions (illusions, auditory/visual hallucinations)
Memory (immediate recall, recent and remote memory)
Judgment about daily living and making reasonable life decisions

IV. Interpersonal relationships (social, emotional functioning)

Present functioning, marriage, job
Interpersonal defenses
Historical, significant figures, conflicts
Quality of relationship to male/female figures
Unconscious material, relevant parental information

V. Self-concept

Statements about self (conscious and unconscious)
Ego strength and self-image

VI. Character structure and diagnosis

Organicity, brain damage
Major defenses (intrapersonal, interpersonal), root conflicts, problems, areas of strength and weakness

VII. Prognosis

Reality factors, environmental
Recommendations for treatment
Prognosis

Chapter 10

A PLANNED APPROACH TO STAFF DEVELOPMENT

The Kikuyu tribe in East Africa epitomizes the concepts of work, growth, and reaping the harvest. They are one of the most productive groups in Africa, and are characterized best by the leadership of Jomo Kenyatta, the late President of Kenya and a Kikuyu spokesperson. The Kikuyu have a proverb that says, "Cia thurguri itiyuraga ikumbi," which interpreted means "do not hope to become rich without cultivating your fields." This proverb can be applied to personnel growth to indicate that a staff can develop personally and professionally as opportunities for growth are cultivated.

Without sufficient opportunities for staff development, counselors can become stagnant. Further, clinical supervision is most effective when combined with a comprehensive program of in-service training and staff development. The latter term refers to a wide range of activities, including preentry training, extramural educational opportunities, ongoing in-service training programs, staff growth experiences, etc. This chapter will address in-service training alternatives, and the agency as a field placement center.

As an introduction to developing a staff training program, there are a number of do's and don'ts for the supervisor.

DO'S	*DON'TS*
1. Do think of training as self-development rather than something done to someone.	1. Don't give counselors more than they can master at any time.
2. Do have the counselor try out what has been learned.	2. Don't misuse fad training methods.
3. Do expose employees to a variety of counseling skills, techniques, and specializations.	3. Don't limit training to so-called high potential staff.
4. Do emphasize the present job as incentives for training.	4. Don't make assumptions about what counselors know.
5. Do use follow-up in supervision, personal attention, recognition of progress and performance.	5. Don't develop isolated training programs which cannot be integrated by staff into an overall system of counseling.
6. Do design systematic, coordinated, comprehensive staff development training programs.	6. Don't seduce counselors into staff development on the faulty basis of career advancement, pay increases, etc.
7. Do develop training curricula that accurately reflects the needs of each person and is consistent with their job functions.	7. Don't make counselor training purely theoretical, devoid of clinical and experiential applications.

8. Do tie training to credentialling requirements for the staff.
9. Do develop small learning goals rather than global ones that are unattainable.

8. Don't try to be all things to all people in training.
9. Don't plead poverty in establishing staff training. There are a number of training experiences that can be offered without large sums of money. To fail to develop a staff training program because of limited funds is doing a disservice to staff and clients.

Staff development is the process of enhancing a worker's performance through planned experiences to meet the present and future performance requirements of the health care delivery system. Other terms that need to be "cleaned up" are institutes, conferences, workshops, short-term intensive courses, etc. In practice, people use these terms interchangeably. Yet, a precise definition offers a source of structure for the trainer and learner. It helps to clarify the trainer–counselor relationship and the expectations of the participants.

Historically, the term, *institute,* is associated with teacher meetings and connotes remedial and "brushing up." The term, however, is used to describe a more formal format that is trainer-controlled with less opportunity for active trainee participation. It stresses information sharing rather than dialogue and skill building. Institutes are traditionally one to three days duration and are frequently the first training offered to a student. The best example of an institute is a summer school for alcohol and drug abuse studies.

Conferences are structured, but less formal, problem-oriented sessions, providing opportunities for active learner participation. Conferences use a greater variety of instructional techniques although the duration of training is similar to that of the institute. Conferences utilize informal settings, such as coffee breaks, banquets, live-in situations, etc., to encourage trainee interaction. Examples of substance abuse conferences are the Annual National Council on Alcoholism Forum and the Alcohol and Drug Problems Association Conference.

Workshops involve the active participation of each trainee. The learning is derived from work assignments and tasks. The trainer is an enabler/facilitator to the group. The workshop is expected to produce a product and is usually of longer duration than institutes or conferences. Smaller groups from the larger trainee population are usually created to enhance group process and dynamics. Short-term courses also fit into this same category, although the latter term is most frequently used to describe formal academic programs.

Many health care institutions are not sensitive to the advantages of in-service education and do not allot the resources and personnel necessary to ensure successful training. The benefits to a program of staff development are numerous:

1. It can supply the necessary ingredients for role proficiency.
2. It provides a structure for educational activities immediately relevant to the needs of the agency and the counselors.
3. Learning is built around agency problems so the application of new learning is immediate and appropriate.
4. It is economically sound as a means of education.
5. It ensures increased performance proficiency.
6. It provides a medium for orienting new employees to the agency.
7. In-service training provides a mechanism to ensure that changes introduced into the agency are adopted.

Staff Development Training Alternatives

In-service training includes a wide range of activities, such as lectures, audiovisual displays, workshops, conferences, didactic presentations, readings, small group discussions, directed individual study, experiential exercises, correspondence study, simulation games, case discussions, grand rounds, etc. In-service training most often occurs with a delimited interdisciplinary group of staff members, within a generalized learning context. The goals are to increase the staff's knowledge base and clinical skills via informational and educational processes. The focus of the sessions tends to be more topically and theoretically oriented than does clinical supervision. In sum, in-service training is distinguished from more specific clinical supervisory sessions by its goals, structure, focus, and methods.

To illustrate these distinctions it is helpful to examine the staff development program of an actual agency: Perth Amboy General Hospital and the Raritan Bay Mental Health Center in New Jersey. Each substance abuse counselor received a minimum of 1 hour of individual clinical supervision per week with the senior counselor. Based upon the issues arising from these sessions, unit-wide in-service training was provided to the 12 staff members on a weekly basis. These 1½ hour sessions addressed common issues of clinical concern for the unit, and for each counselor. Occasionally, live presentations were used as teaching tools, but the primary focus of the sessions was upon general topical concerns. The content for the in-service training was delivered via didactic presentations.

Additionally, each treatment unit of the program participated in weekly agency-wide in-service training (1½ hours per session). These sessions addressed broad mental health issues, such as confidentiality, recordkeeping, fee setting, psychopathology, community organization, volunteerism, and legal issues of clients.

Finally, each unit was responsible for its own case management procedures. Weekly administrative sessions were held for

1 hour to ensure the efficient flow of clients throughout the system. Agency-wide staffing and case presentations were made weekly for all incoming clients.

Each of these sessions was essential to the development of the staff and the operation of the program. To eliminate any one component would be to disturb the agency's staff development program and clinical operations.

What Makes a Good Staff Development Program?

1. To be effective, training must be relevant to the needs of the learner group. The curriculum must be based on the results of a valid needs assessment survey and discrepancy analysis. It must be meaningful to the staff for their daily operations, and have practical applicability for the counselors' functioning.
2. In-service training should be comprehensive in scope and systematic in planning. It should be well organized, encompassing the range of staff training needs. It should be planned in advance and should be organized for optimally one year prior to delivery.
3. Training must have clear, measurable behavioral objectives for the course of study. These objectives should state what the learner will be able to do that she is unable to do now. In what context will the action occur? The old maxim must be examined, "If it is not worth doing, it is not worth doing well."

   Stating behavioral objectives involves defining the conditions and behaviors to be changed, what the learner will be doing in the training, how will success be recognized, and how will one know how well he did. Desirability and feasibility criteria should be examined in establishing behavioral objectives: the emerging career directions of the counselors, the extent to which the objectives can realistically be achieved within a given time frame, the availability of resources to assist, and the counselors' own commitment to achieve the objectives before this can occur, however, there are preliminary steps to be taken: formulation and enunciation of the philosphy of the treatment program itself, and clarification of the learning goals in relation to what the agency is, what it believes in, and how it deals with clientele.

4. In-service training must be placed in an appropriate position in the organization and staffed with people in order to carry out its assigned functions. It has traditionally been lodged with the personnel department which is not a suitable position in the organizational structure. Personnel departments are often placed in a line position in the hierarchy and are considered to be in a rather lowly status in the pecking order, As a result, the educational director finds herself with both minimal prestige, low authority, and a nominal salary.

   Also, by having in-service training as part of the activities of the personnel department, staff may view education as an unimportant agency priority and not worth taking seriously. Rather, in-service training should be a separate entity located in a position independent of personnel. This may be a moot point in a smaller alcoholism or drug abuse agency. However, wherever possible, in-service training should be viewed and established as a separate and distinct system.

5. In-service training should be just that: training. The trainer should be able to communicate with all levels of manpower and able to develop creative responses to learning needs. If possible, this person should have exposure to training of trainer workshops to emphasize the principles and practices of adult learning.

6. Learning in alcoholism agencies should have a cognitive and affective orientation. Instruction should not be limited to the dissemination of information. Cognitive objectives may also include the development of principles by combining bits of information, establishing relationships among them, and problem-solving. Affective learning involves objectives related to attitudes, feelings, interests, and emotions.
7. In-service training should be based on sound instructional processes incorporating the following ideas:

Learning is an active process and adults prefer to participate actively.

Group learning is more effective than individual learning.

Learning applied immediately is retained longer than that which is not.

Learning new material is facilitated when it is related to what is already known.

Learning is facilitated when the learner is aware of his progress (see Tables 4 and 5).

Scheduling, payroll, mailing and telephone privileges/restrictions, absentee procedures, compensatory time, holidays, vacations, sick time, health insurance benefits, etc.

Familiarization with the various other staff development components, such as clinical supervision, in-service training, and extramural training, opportunities, etc.

An introduction to agency recordkeeping procedures, confidentiality regulations, standards for ethical and professional practice, procedures for case flow, evaluations and assessment procedures, teaching responsibilities, client tracking procedures, case management policies, accountability, etc.

Table 4. Tactics, Settings, and Dimensions of Training*

Tactics	*Settings*	*Dimensions*
Telling	Classroom	Guidance
Showing	Laboratory	Activity
Critiquing	Clinic	Reality

* From Maier, Norman R. F. Three types of appraisal interview. *The appraisal interview.* New York: Wiley, 1958, p. 40.

Too many program directors/trainers make the invalid assumption that new personnel (because they are professionals) have basic knowledge in all of these areas. However, even if they do, a restatement of agency policies and procedures is helpful to ensure a common understanding of these issues among all personnel.

8. The "bibliography" of in-service training should combine a variety of items, including readings, "homework" assignments, bibliographies, videotape viewing, etc.
9. Instructional strategies should reflect the setting, dimensions, and tactics of training (Table 4). The advantages of these various tactics should also be explored.
10. In-service training should make good utilization of self-instructional methods. It is not an efficient use of the trainer's time to devote his efforts to dispensing information in ways that could be done through self-instructional materials. The merits of such units are determined by their objectives, clarity of presentation, learner activities, and feedback mechanisms. There are few suitable self-instructional packages available in the substance abuse field, and even fewer in the area of counselor skill development. However, there are a number of sound introductions to alcoholism and drug abuse. A skilled in-service trainer can combine an acceptable bibliography of existing materials.

Table 5. Advantages and Disadvantages of Various Tactics*

Tactics	*Advantages*	*Disadvantages*
Telling	Saves time and trouble; is inexpensive because it's group-oriented	Is superficial or confusing; ultimately students must actually do
Showing	Avoids serious problems; gives goals for students	Is small-group oriented; ultimately students must actually do
Critiquing	Allows students to actually do; gives fresh feedback	Is expensive because of individual orientation

* From Maier, Norman R. F. Three types of appraisal interview, *The appraisal interview*. New York: Wiley, 1958, p. 41.

11. Quality in-service training can be developed with minimal funding through the appropriate use of favors, "freebees," interagency sharing, etc. To plead poverty either displays one's ignorance of the resources or a demonstration of inertia and sloth. The old saying applies here, "A wise man knows everything, but a shrewd man knows everyone." As a director develops her program, there are an increasing number of contacts made with other health care agencies. This is enhanced if the program is part of an overall treatment system, such as a community mental health center or general hospital. Such contacts can be utilized in sharing speakers and other resource materials. Interagency in-service training is possible. "If you stroke my back, I'll stroke yours," by mutually sharing staff development training opportunities. The Alcoholism Treatment Program of Perth Amboy General Hospital in New Jersey was able to conduct a full year of comprehensive in-service training for a staff of 25 persons by exchanging resources from within and without the system.

Additionally, there are a number of "freebees" available through the Department of Health, Education and Welfare, and the various state offices. Handouts, booklets, texts, bibliographical materials, etc. are all available generally at no expense. From the federal alphabet soup, here are a few of these resources:

National Center for Alcohol Education (NCAE)
National Center for Child Abuse (NCCA)
National Clearinghouses for Alcohol and Drug Abuse Information (NCALI)
National Institute of Mental Health (NIMH)
National Center for Voluntary Action (NCVA)
National Organization for Planned Parenthood (NOPP)
The National Institute on Alcohol Abuse and Alcoholism, and the National Institute on Drug Abuse (NIAAA,-NIDA)

The state alcohol and drug abuse authority also has available films and publications for use by community programs, as does the state and local library system and local colleges. Many states also have training modules available to their service delivery agencies, such as the training funded by the National Institute on Drug Abuse (NIDA) through the Regional Support Centers. Funds for training are also available from Title XX, CETA, etc. Training packages are provided by the Regional Support Centers in the following areas:

Counselor skills
Long-term treatment planning
Confidentiality and professional ethics
Legal issues
Assessment interviewing
Women in treatment

Third party reimbursement
Methadone management
Vocational rehabilitation counseling
Impacting on youth
Management skills
Emergency treatment
Criminal justice systems

The National Center for Alcohol Education has training packages in the following areas:

Women and alcohol
Use of volunteers
Counselor skills
Programming community resources
The role of the public health nurse
Management skills
Primary prevention programming
Training of trainers
Decisions and drinking

These packages are available at no cost to the agency, and with the NIDA programs, the training is delivered by the Regional Support Center staff at no expense to the treatment organizations. In sum, there are numerous sources of "free" training available to local agencies. A wise program administrator/trainer will make use of all of these resources.

12. Staff development programs should also utilize extramural training resources, combined into a comprehensive system (Fig. 14):

Academic programs
Schools of alcohol and drug abuse studies

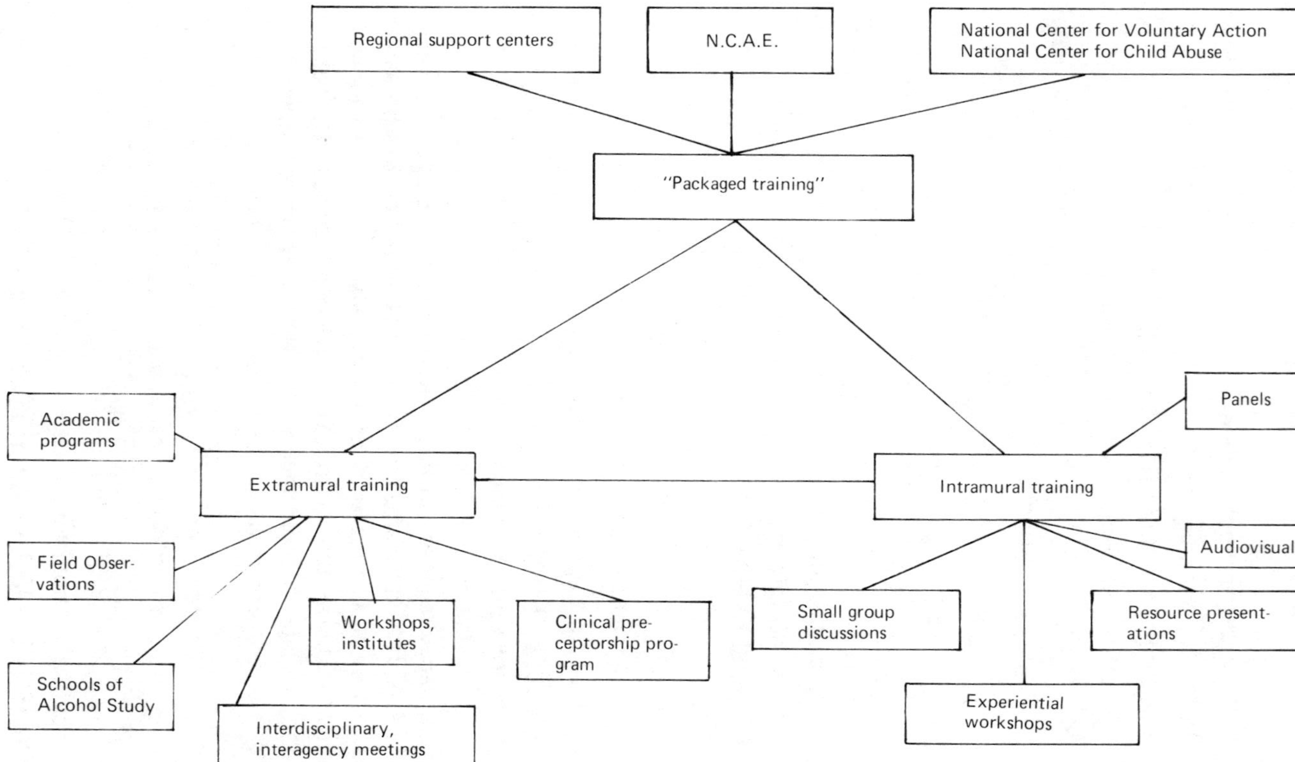

Fig. 14. Staff development training system.

Field observations at "sister" agencies and other health care delivery systems

Conferences, workshops, seminars, etc.

The Clinical Preceptorship Program of the Eastern Area Alcohol Education and Training Program (see Appendix B)

Interdisplinary group meetings; most larger areas have interagency councils which provide an orientation to the broad range of health care agencies.

Although it is cost effective to provide education and training on-site, and to maximize the intramural training opportunities, staff should be encouraged to paticipate in extramural training programs. This promotes a sense of growth, exchange, and sharing between agencies. It also allows for a certain amount of needed staff rest and relaxation time, away from the demands of the job site.

13. Staff development programs should also provide an orientation component to new workers, and an opportunity to present changes and modifications in the program to all personnel. Regardless of the background, every new staff member should be introduced to the agency, his role, and his responsibilities. Counselors may have some familiarity with the goals of health care in general but need to familiarize themselves with the specific operations of the new agency.

Orientation programs should include these elements:

An introduction to the agency, its goals, standard operating procedures, and regulations affecting personnel

Familiarization with the general physical layout and the various departments, if applicable

An introduction to the specific responsibilities and authority of the job, the personnel with whom the new worker will be having contact, etc.

An introduction to lines of authority in the agency

An introduction to administrative issues, such as working hours, absentee procedures, vacations, sick time, holidays, mail and phone privileges and restrictions, etc.

Your Agency as a Field Placement Center

The optimal "classroom" for learning counselor skills is the actual clinical setting. A trainee learns by doing as she tries out her counseling theories and techniques in realistic situations. The clinical laboratory becomes the testing grounds for skill development. Field experience is not a "tacking on" to training. It is the essential ingredient in enhancing the entire learning experience of a counselor.

Why should an agency open their doors to novice counselors to "learn the trade?" What benefits are there to the agency as compared to the expenditures of staff time and energy in supervising the student? What is in it for the agency?

1. Students working in an agency provide a stimulating freshness for the clinical staff: new ideas are explored, old methods are questioned, and stagnation is combated. A sense of energy and enthusiasm is present whenever trainees are involved.
2. Growth stimulates growth. Students challenge staff to constantly examine and evaluate themselves: what role models are being provided, are they always acting in the best interest of the clients, is the agency providing the highest quality of care possible?
3. If a student is in residence for any significant period of time, he is able to assume some clinical responsibilities, thus relieving some of the pressures on other staff.

Although this is abused in agencies, where internships are perceived as a form of "cheap labor," if used discriminately, students can serve as valuable members of the clinical team.

4. Contact with students and external training centers guards against an insularity by an agency because participation with other systems is involved. For example, frequently practicums at agencies involve contact with colleges and universities, a valuable process for small, isolated programs.
5. The treatment center becomes known as a training ground with qualified teaching staff. This increases the potential of the program to seduce capable counselors to the staff. The reputation of the program is enhanced; recruitment of highly qualified counseling staff is made easier.

When a treatment program wishes to offer field placements to counselor trainees, they can expect a number of general things from the students: Observation of all agency rules and regulations concerning attendance, administrative procedures, participation in agency functions, punctuality, dress codes (if applicable), etc. Sufficient recordkeeping on assigned cases are to be maintained. Attendance at all regularly scheduled clinical supervisory sessions is required. Appropriate professional and ethical behavior is to be maintained. An active role in the ongoing evaluation process is desirable. Students should participate in all clinical functions (individual, group, family counseling, etc.) as assigned.

As a field placement site the agency is expected to:

Provide an orientation to the agency to all trainees, including an introduction to the facilities, role expectation, policies and procedures, recordkeeping methodologies, how the trainee should title himself, etc.

Provide sufficient office space and administrative/clerical support to properly perform the duties assigned. If a student is expected to conduct individual counseling sessions, office space must be provided at the same level as would be given to other clinical staff.

Expect of the student the highest standards of professional and ethical conduct as well as clinical functioning. Although this may appear to be a requirement of the student, the agency itself must have standards which they can present to the student.

Provide regularly scheduled clinical supervisory sessions, and other training opportunities. As a rule of thumb for field placements, one hour of clinical supervision should be provided for every 4 to 5 client contact hours.

Regularly evaluate and discuss the critique with the student.

Have a clinical supervisor specifically identified and assigned to each trainee. The clinical supervisor must be available for formal and informal student conferences.

Help the student to plan his schedule so that the maximum opportunity for learning occurs.

Acknowledge to staff the trainee at the onset of training and throughout the learning process.

To maximize the training opportunities of a treatment program, a minimum period for the placements should be established. It is hardly cost effective for an agency to accept students for shorter than a 3-month period. The majority of the student's first few months are spent in orientation and observation. There is an inordinate amount of drain on an agency with short-term (1–3 months) placements. It is helpful for an agency to set an absolute minimum period of months (6) for internships, with an optimal period of 12 months. This allows for cases to be assigned to trainees and for the student to maintain these cases throughout the treatment program. To do otherwise is a disservice to the agency, the trainee, and most importantly, to the client.

During the supervisory experience, minimum requirements should be established for trainees, depending on their individual training needs and abilities. In a 6-month placement, trainees should be required to do at least the following:

- 10 intakes with detailed reports and progress notes
- 5 case presentations before staff
- Coordinate treatment plans for all assigned cases, including making referrals when necessary
- Conduct as leader and/or coleader 52 hours of supervised individual counseling, 52 hours of supervised group counseling, and/or 52 hours of family counseling, depending upon the services provided by the agency and the skills of the counselor/trainee
- 6 educational presentations to clients, and 2 educational presentations to community groups as part of the consultation and education component of the treatment program
- Spend 1 week in a hospital emergency room, and 2 days in a detoxification facility, if applicable.
- Familiarize themselves with various health care delivery resources within the community
- Do outside readings and assignments as the clinical supervisor sees necessary to augment the learning experience

Too many treatment agencies limit the clinical responsibilities of trainees to only clinical observations and not direct client contact. To do so is to severely cripple the learning potential for the agency and the trainee. If field observation is the best an agency can offer, this must be clear to all involved, the trainee, the supervisor, the training center, etc.

From the outset the clinical supervisor should explain the structure of the training to be provided; the frequency, length, and location of all staff and clinical supervisory meetings; the materials expected of the trainee; and the records to be kept.

Not all treatment agencies can or should become training centers and field placement sites. They must be carefully selected on the following basis:

The number and availability of skilled clinical supervisors who can provide clinical training to students

Their ability to integrate knowledge and skills in practical experiences

The variety of their client population and the availability of cases to be assigned to trainees

Their other teaching capabilities, including in-service, and extramural training opportunities.

In selecting clinical supervisors to serve as field placement supervisors, a number of criteria should be utilized:

The formal and informal training background of the person, including experience and training in the theory and practice of counseling

The ability of the person to impart information and skills to others

Affability and ability to establish rapport with students

Someone who is currently engaged in practice with at least 3 to 5 years of clinical experience; ("Know how to do it yourself before you try to teach others.")

Ability to be open with one's own feelings, and able to share these with others

Ability to criticize the professional behavior of himself and others

A background in the substance abuse field, including a familiarity with the nature and extent of alcohol and drug abuse and appropriate methods of care and treatment

To be effective as a training center, the agency should have the right to screen and select all trainees, based on their perceptions of the students and their agency's needs. To accept anyone into a practicum is to reduce the potential of individualized instruction based on the strengths and weaknesses of the placement agency and the trainee.

Chapter 11

CONCLUSION

Paul Tillich (1966), the famous theologian, begins his autobiography by stating that "the boundary is the best place for acquiring knowledge." Even as Tillich describes his life as living "on the boundary" between various polarities, even so the concept of the boundary is a fitting symbol for the whole of the personal, professional, and intellectual development of alcoholism and drug abuse counselors. At virtually every point, counselors find themselves positioned between a number of alternatives and polarities that determine the future direction of the field.

The counselor is comfortable in neither polarity and yet required to grow and change. This book has addressed a number of the alternatives available to the counselor. The book examined the role of the clinical supervisor in aiding the counselor in coping with the creative tension of living "on the boundary."

The polarities for the counselor and the clinical supervisor highlighted in this book are summarized as lying between the following:

Dependence and independence; heteronomy and autonomy

Substance abuse as a separate entity or integrated into the health care delivery mainstream

Clinical supervison vs. psychotherapy

Theory and practice

Idealism and pragmatism

Spontaneity vs. "trained responsiveness"

Being a "boss" vs. a friend

Being a supervisor to some and a supervisee to others

Client vs. counselor vs. agency rights

Tillich states that the man who stands on many boundaries [as does the alcoholism and drug abuse counselor] experiences the unrest, insecurity, and inner limitations inherent to that position. Possibilities of attaining a sense of security and serenity are limited by the degree of internal dialectic experienced and the resources available to the individual to cope with and overcome the constraints of the "boundary" tension. The clinical supervisor is the most vital link in this resource chain for the counselor. He can aid the counselor "on the boundary" in his personal and professional growth and evolution as a helping agent.

The most crucial issue confronting the substance abuse field today appears to be whether its constituency will be able to move from being an appendage to the larger mental health field, to becoming part of the mainstream of health care delivery in the United States. The role of the alcoholism and drug abuse counselor in this assimilation is the key question. As Dr. Blume states in the Foreword to this book, counseling and Twelve Stepping the client are not synonymous. The clinical skills of the counselors in the field must be upgraded if the alcoholism and drug abuse counselor is to reach parity with other mental health disciplines.

The day in which the counselor will be able to continue to live "on the boundary" is limited. Only as the quality of clinical training provided to the counselor is improved, as the extent and quality of clinical supervisory experiences are expanded, will the field be able to stand as an equal among the other disciplines.

This book has provided an overview of clinical supervision, its definition, principles and practices. No textbook, though, can make a person a counselor, or a clinical supevisor. The key to being a supervisor is to be exposed as a trainee to quality clinical supervision. With the theoretical background provided in this book, and the experience of having been supervised, one must learn as any counselor in training learns: by doing.

Appendix A

A JOB DESCRIPTION FOR A CLINICAL SUPERVISOR IN THE SUBSTANCE ABUSE FIELD

Experience

A minimum of four (4) years of experience in the field of mental health, with a minimum of two (2) years of time in the field of substance abuse would be required. The experience ought to include a minimum of two (2) years of clinical practice, involving individual, family, and group counseling with alcoholics and/or drug abusers and their spouses. The supervisor ought to possess a thorough knowledge of the principles and concepts of psychopathology and group dynamics. A minimum of one (1) year of the above time ought to be in the capacity of a clinical supervisor. He ought also to have experience in alcoholism education and staff development programs.

Education

Graduation from an accredited college or university with courses in psychology and/or counseling would be required.

Also, graduation from an approved graduate course of study with courses in the area of individual and/or group counseling, social case work, and/or community organization.

Responsibilities

1. Provides supervision to the counselors of the agency; promotes and maintains quality health care delivery by serving as a role model in his interactions with patients and personnel
2. Initiates and implements those practices which lead to quality health care
3. Assesses the degree of stress and brings into action the kinds of services that help a patient make the most effective use of care through interviews with the patient and significant others
4. Helps the client to mobilize his resources and those of the community in the use of the patient care
5. Participates in community activities relating to health and welfare services
6. Is responsible for influencing the policies, procedures, and personnel of the agency towards eliminating those factors that add to patient stress and hinder the effective delivery of services
7. Develops standards for performance for the staff and initiates innovations in the roles of staff in keeping within the legal and professional codes and current developments in the field
8. Assists in appraising performance, recommending salary changes, discharges, disciplinary actions, and other personnel procedures as necessary
9. Serves as a role model for other staff members and clients by implementing his knowledge of interpersonal relationships, communications theory and systems approaches, in his interactions with these individuals

10. Assists in the coordination of staff development training programs
11. Interprets the philosophy, principles, and practices of the treatment agency to other programs and serves as a consultant to such services

Abilities and Skills

1. To possess a thorough knowledge of the problem being treated, its etiology, epidemiology, treatment, and prevention
2. Familiarity with the philosophy, approaches, and resources of the local, state, and national organizations which deal with the problems of alcoholism and/or drug abuse
3. The ability to relate to the patients in a constructive manner and to be able to establish a therapeutic rapport with them
4. To possess the knowledge and skills and to design and carry out a treatment plan for his assigned clients in the treatment modality which seems appropriate
5. To possess skills in individual, family, and group psychotherapy as well as casework
6. To possess the knowledge of the principles of psychopathology, psychodynamics, intrapsychic issues, group dynamics, family systems, etc., as well as the basic principles and techniques of psychotherapy of the major schools of treatment
7. The ability to relate this knowledge to his practice and his peers
8. Familiarity with the community organizations and other treatment services in the geographic area of the agency and to constructively work with these organizations and agencies
9. Familiarity with the theoretical changes that affect the delivery of health care and the agencies' response

to these changes, and the methods and means for implementing that response

10. To possess the knowledge of educational techniques and the skills to design and carry out a program of staff development for other staff
11. To possess skills in organization and supervision, displaying the ability to coordinate and direct subordinates
12. Familiarity with the basic concepts of staff development and training, and the ability and skill to utilize that information

Appendix B

EASTERN AREA ALCOHOL EDUCATION AND TRAINING PROGRAM'S CLINICAL PRECEPTORSHIP PROGRAM

Background

The need for education and training experiences has been expressed by counselors and employers. Several kinds of training programs have evolved to respond to this need. There are, however, major obstacles to potential participants:

The costs involved in attending a residential training program (travel, per diem, and tuition).

The length of the training session which leaves the employer shortstaffed.

The hardship on some counselors to be away from home for extended periods.

Frequently, the training does not address the educational needs of the counselor or the employing agency.

These limitations must be considered in the development of an educational model designed to enhance the knowledge and skills of the employed alcoholism counselor. The characteristics of the adult learner also must be considered in developing a sound educational experience. An envisioned training program for the employed counselor should be based on the following assumptions:

Alcoholism counselors tend to be laypersons, without formal academic training that prepared them for their position.

Minimal staff time can be allocated to the training. The counselor cannot be released for extended periods.

The employer or the alcoholism program director may not be a counselor. He may be an administrator or a professional therapist.

Frequently, the employee's supervisor has limited experience in providing clinical supervision.

Counselors are motivated to improve their skills and to be prepared for credentialling.

The EAAETP Needs Assessment Survey indicates the number one training need in the alcoholism field in the Eastern area to be skill development training of an advanced nature for alcoholism counselors. The study further suggests a lack of adequate clinical supervision being provided to those in the field (over one-half of the 1000 respondents stated that they received no clinical supervision). This points to the need for the development of a plan to improve the quality and quantity of clinical supervision for alcoholism counselors.

Several educational models are possible to meet this need; however, to address the concerns, limitations, and assumptions stated above, a Clinical Preceptorship Program seems to be an optimal approach.

Description of the Clinical Preceptorship Program

The EAAETP Clinical Preceptorship Program is intended to provide in-depth clinical supervision to alcoholism counselors, and a much needed system of advanced skill development training, minimizing the above limitations and restrictions. The basic educational method is one-to-one and small group clinical supervision.

Rationale for the Program

The Clinical Preceptorship Program provides a system for advanced clinical training for counselors that was previously unavailable. The training is personalized to meet the needs of each trainee and provides practical clinical skill building. The Program offers the trainee a close working relationship and learning experience with a clinical supervisor, outside of the work setting, in an atmosphere in which the trainee can take risks and openly share clinical experiences and problems. The training will further assist the trainee in his/her career development and in meeting part of the requirements for counselor certification in many states.

The advantage of the EAAETP conducting the Clinical Preceptorship Program is that area-wide coordination of the program will be maintained. The trainee and the preceptor will receive recognition for the experience across state lines with the EAAETP Board of Directors providing quality control and assurance that the best possible training is being provided.

For preceptors, the training program provides key individuals the opportunity to be involved in an innovative approach which provides skilled professionals to the field, and ultimately, improves the quality of care received by the alcoholic patient.

Who are the Clinical Preceptors?

The Accreditation and Clinical Training Committee of the EAAETP has established a network of clinical preceptors in each state throughout the Eastern area. These EAAETP-approved clinical preceptors are individuals with demonstrated expertise in the field of alcoholism, experienced in providing clinical services to alcoholics, and who have clinical supervisory experience. The following criteria for clinical preceptors is utilized:

1. The person must have a minimum of 5 years of experience as a clinician, with 2 of the 5 years as a clinical supervisor.
2. Two of the 5 years are to be in working with a caseload in which at least 50 percent of the clients were alcoholics.
3. A minimum number of 3 years of approved full-time clinical supervision in the practice of counseling.
4. The preceptor must be familiar with recent developments in the alcohol field.
5. The clinical preceptors must possess at least a Master's degree in a relevant behavioral science field, *or have equivalent stature in the field* as determined by the EAAETP Accreditation and Clinical Training Committee.
6. The preceptor must be a practicing clinician, either of a full-time, part-time, or private practice nature.
7. The individual must have made a significant contribution to the field of alcoholism, with a demonstrated advanced level of clinical competence and experience, as determined by the EAAETP Accreditation and Clinical Training Committee.
8. The clinical preceptor is required to have a screening

interview with the EAAETP Accreditation and Clinical Training Committee. The preceptor may be requested to submit a case analysis and description as part of the application process.

How Does One Become a Clinical Preceptor?

Individuals may request, in writing, Clinical Preceptor status. An application form is to be completed by the individual and reviewed by the EAAETP Accreditation and Clinical Training Committee.

A limited number of clinical preceptors are selected per state. This number is based upon geographic restraints, population density, the demand for training, and the availability of qualified candidates. The actual number of clinical preceptors is determined by the Accreditation and Clinical Training Committee in concert with the State Alcoholism Authority.

The prospective preceptor is required to participate in a one-day training session, conducted at a central geographic location, at which time a Guide for Preceptors is distributed and discussed. Having completed this training, he/she can then commence providing training under the aegis of the EAAETP. Names of EAAETP-approved clinical preceptors are designated in appropriate notices and publications of the EAAETP. Certificates are also issued to the preceptors.

How Does the Clinical Preceptorship Program Operate?

1. Trainees apply directly to the EAAETP for approval to begin a program of advanced clinical training under the supervision of an EAAETP-approved clinical preceptor. The Accreditation and Clinical Training Committee of the EAAETP acts upon the application and, if approved, recommends geographically convenient clinical preceptors. The choice of a preceptor remains that of the trainee, except in some cases in

which the Committee might specify a particular preceptor to meet the needs of a trainee.

2. The individual then contacts the clinical preceptor and arranges an introductory interview to discuss a possible training schedule.

3. The Clinical Preceptorship Program provides a minimum of 50 hours of in-depth personalized clinical supervision to each trainee over a one-year period. The specific scheduling is determined by the trainee and the preceptor. Individual sessions last for 50 minutes and group sessions from 1½ to 2 hours. Each trainee will receive a minimum of 18 hours of *individual* clinical supervision. The remaining 32 hours of training can be in group supervision sessions of 2 to 4 trainees.

4. The 50 hours of training will be completed in no less than 30 weeks and no more than 52 weeks.

5. Since an essential ingredient to the Clinical Preceptorship Program is contact of the trainee with actual clients, it is necessary that the trainee be employed in a program or agency in which he/she has direct contact with clients and is involved in a counseling relationship with a number of these clients, or have access to clients through contractual agreements with a service agency or the preceptor.

6. During the clinical supervisory sessions, the preceptor discusses with the trainee(s) case studies with which the individual is involved. This may require videotaping of sessions, plus verbatims and case reviews of client progress. It is recommended that the sessions focus upon the progress of one or two clients whom the trainee may be involved with in therapy over an extended period of time.

7. The training will be conducted at the location selected by the preceptor, preferably at his/her site or facility. In the case of an agency which has two or more trainees involved in the Clinical Preceptorship Program, arrangements can be made with the preceptor to have the training conducted at the agency site.

Who are the Trainees?

The trainees in the Clinical Preceptorship Program are individuals in the field of alcoholism who have responsibilities in their employment for the direct care and treatment of clients, or who have access to clients through contractual agreements with a service agency or the preceptor. Further, the trainee is to be employed in a position in which his/her *primary job responsibility* is client-oriented, counseling-related. Those in solely clerical or administrative positions would be ineligible.

The Clinical Preceptorship Program is an advanced training experience and should be undertaken by those who already have basic and necessary knowledge concerning alcohol and alcoholism, gathered through either life experiences, reading, and/or treatment experiences. Although individuals may have attended other training programs, the Preceptorship Program provides intensive training of a sort that is rarely received in basic courses of study. Thus, this Program does not duplicate or supplant existing training.

The trainee should have the following knowledge base before entering the Clinical Preceptorship Program:

1. Basic alcohol and alcoholism information
   - Physiology and pharmacology of alcohol
   - Effects of alcohol on the body
   - Psychological and sociocultural issues related to alcohol and alcoholism
   - Knowledge of signs and symptoms of alcoholism
   - Identification of alcoholics
   - Other alcohol-related problems

2. Counseling
   - Human growth and development
   - Normal human behavior principles, including family dynamics and interaction

Nonverbal behavior
Overview of predominant theoretical approaches to counseling
Client intake procedures
Facilitative counseling conditions

3. Programs for alcoholics and their significant others
   Concepts of the continuum of care
   The available services for alcoholics
   Community resource utilization

What Expenses are involved for the Trainee?

The trainee is expected to pay a fee for the experience. Each trainee would be charged a maximum of $850.00 per year for the training. Because of the individual and personalized nature of the Clinical Preceptorship Program, this fee is most reasonable. This fee would be paid by the trainee or his employer to the EAAETP on a monthly, quarterly, or yearly basis, depending upon the availability of funds. Employers of trainees are encouraged to assume part of the expense, since the trainee's agency will receive skill development training for that individual, and ultimately, a more skilled employee at the completion of the training.

The clinical preceptor will be reimbursed by the EAAETP on a quarterly basis for the consultation services provided to the trainee in this program.

How will the Program be Monitored?

The EAAETP Accreditation and Clinical Training Committee and staff will closely monitor the Program through consulation with the preceptors and the trainees, and a follow-up survey of trainees and possibly his/her employer. The preceptor must submit quarterly statements to the EAAETP on each trainee, including a summary of the number of individual and group supervisory sessions provided to each trainee during that quarter; a completed evaluation of each trainee's progress; at least two tapes of a preceptorship training session, one at the beginning and the other near the completion of the training; at least one case record done by each trainee; and, an audio tape of the evaluation processing session between preceptor and trainee. A peer review on each trainee will also be conducted.

Efforts are made to tie the training into the needs of the trainee's employer, thus ensuring relevant experiences for the students.

The individual, at the completion of the training experiences, receives a certificate assuring the employee and his/her employer of comparability and standardization of training. The Clinical Preceptorship Program is being incorporated into the various State Alcoholism Counselor certification and licensing standards and into a number of State Civil Service Systems as meeting the requirements for certification, licensing, or employment.

CURRICULUM

The Clinical Preceptorship model for alcoholism counselor preparation addresses two curriculum issues: The counselor role and skill development.

The Counselor Role

The key concept in the counselor role is the professional responsibilities that the counselor takes on as an agency employee providing human services. Included in this concept is an understanding of confidentiality, ethics, accountability, professional behavior, legal implications, relationships with other service providers, and other distinctions between voluntarily providing services and being an agency employee. The counselor must understand himself, his attitudes towards his clients, and his expectations of the counselor role. He must base his actions on objective, accurate knowledge. In professional schools this material is communicated in formal courses. In the Clinical Preceptorship Program this content is presented informally through communications between the clinical preceptor and the trainee.

Skill Development

The area of alcoholism counselor preparation that is crucial to functioning in the field, but is often minimally addressed in curricula, is the development of clinical skills. Most education and training programs in alcoholism provide the necessary knowledge base underlying the clinical skills. Training, though, must also be concerned with demonstration and practice of these competencies.

The Clinical Preceptorship Program provides a curriculum for alcoholism counselors with appropriate skill development training. The Program focuses upon the various skills which a counselor should have. Alcoholism counselors perform a number of tasks in their delivery of client services. Task refers to a cluster of work functions that jointly form a specific clinical intervention. Associated with these tasks are a series of competencies identified as part of the profile for each task. Competency is defined as the skills and knowledge required to perform a particular task. Each competency profile should include a definition of the task, a range of various functions involved in that task, and competencies needed to effectively accomplish the task.

The following are the clinical tasks which an alcoholism counselor is generally responsible for:

1. Intake and client assessment
2. Assisting in developing a treatment plan
3. Individual, family, and group counseling
4. Continuous evaluation of client progress

5. Crisis intervention counseling
6. Client follow-up contact, patient tracking, and referral
7. Seeking and using collateral support (employer, friends, etc.)
8. Coordination of the treatment plan

In order to perform these tasks, it is necessary that an alcoholism counselor possess certain skills or competencies. The curriculum of the Clinical Preceptorship Program focuses upon a number of skills to include, but not be limited to, the following:

1. Affective qualities, such as empathy, concreteness, self-actualization, respect, genuineness, congruence, and confrontation
2. Skills in assessing the stage of alcoholism found in the client and client needs
3. Case history methodology skills
4. Skills in developing a treatment plan and in working through client reactions and resistances to this plan
5. Skills in making a referral should additional services be needed for the client
6. Skills in establishing a genuine therapeutic relationship with the client
7. Ability to conceptualize the therapeutic relationship
8. Ability to use counseling techniques to elicit feelings, facilitate self-understanding, and motivate the client
9. Skills in individual, family, and group counseling methods
10. Ability to participate in and coordinate a client's continuum of treatment
11. Ability to participate in various in-patient and out-patient treatment processes; knowledge of their relationship, methods, and limitation
12. Ability to justify therapeutic interventions
13. Ability to maintain the necessary safeguards to en-

sure confidentiality of clients and ethical standards for clinical practice
14. Skills in assisting clients in recognizing and solving problems precipitated by alcohol abuse
15. Ability to terminate a counseling session and treatment plan
16. Ability to prepare and conduct aftercare activities for the client
17. Skills in maintaining client reports and records

These skills and competencies will be monitored and evaluated by the EAAETP Accreditation and Clinical Training Committee through the administration of preceptor evaluation forms and reports from the trainee's employer.

Summary

One of the important needs in the alcohol field is the skill development training of a cadre of individuals who can provide appropriate services to the alcoholic and his/her family. This is also one of the most pressing issues as certification standards are established. In order to meet this need for training, the EAAETP is establishing a network of clinical trainers for alcoholism counselors, wherein individuals in the field can receive skill development training under close clinical supervision with an EAAETP-approved preceptor. This training would be carried out within the trainee's locale, thus requiring a minimum of travel and expense. Through this plan, the level of expertise in the field will be upgraded and will ultimately result in improvements in the quality of care provided to those in need.

BIBLIOGRAPHY

Abrahamson, A. C. *Group methods in supervision and staff development.* New York: Harper, 1959.

American Psychological Association. Internship in clinical psychology. *American Psychologist,* 1954, *9,* 760–64.

Apaka, T. K., Hirsch, S., & Kleidman, S. Establishing group supervision in a hospital social work department. *Social Work,* 1967, *12,* 54–60.

Armstrong, M., & Spain, M. *The use of process tape recordings as tools in learning casework.* M.A. Thesis, Sioux City, State University of Iowa, 1959.

Bach, G. R., & Wyden, P. *The Intimate Enemy.* New York: William Morrow, 1966.

Bauman, W. F. Games counselor trainees play: Dealing with trainee resistance. *Counselor Education and Supervision,* 1972, *12,* 251–57.

Beiser, H. Self-history during supervision of psychotherapy. *Archives of General Psychiatry,* 1966, *15,* 135–39.

Benschoter, R. A., Eaton, M. T., & Smith, D. 1965. Use of videotape to provide individual instruction in techniques of psychotherapy. *Journal of Medical Education,* 1965, *40,* 1159–61.

Blackey, E. *Group leadership in staff training.* Bureau of Public Assistance. H.E.W. Report # 29. Washington, D.C.: U.S. Government Printing Office, 1957.

Blake, R. R., & Mouton, S. S. *The managerial grid.* Houston: Gulf, 1961.

Blume, S. B. *Confidentiality of medical records in alcohol-related problems.* New York: National Council on Alcoholism, Inc., 1976.

Blume, S. B. The role of the recovered alcoholic in the treatment of alcoholism. In B. Kissin & H. Begleiter. *The biology of alcoholism* (Vol. 5) New York: Plenum Press, 1977.

Boylston, W. H., & Tuma, J. M. Training of mental health professionals through the use of the 'bug in the ear.' *American Journal of Psychiatry,* 1972, *129,* 92–95.

Brown, C. R. Mandatory continuing education: Sense of nonsense. *Journal of American Medical Association,* 1970, *213,* 1660–8.

Brugger, T., Ceasor, G., & Martz, S. Peer supervision as a method of learning psychotherapy. *Comprehensive Psychiatry, 1962, 3,* 47–53.

Carkhuff, R. R., & Berenson, B. G. *Beyond counseling and therapy.* New York: Holt, 1967.

Carkhuff, R. R., & Truax, C. B. Training in counseling and psychotherapy: An evaluation of an integrated didactic and experiential approach. *Journal of Consulting Psychology,* 1965, *29,* 333–336.

Chodoff, P. Supervision of psychotherapy with video-tape: pros and cons. *American Journal of Psychiatry,* 1972, *128,* 819–23.

Code of ethics for professional alcoholism counselors. Adapted from NIAAA Proposed Standards for Alcoholism Counselors by the Clinical Standards Committee of the Regional Training Program for Alcoholism Counselors, The Johns Hopkins University, Baltimore, Md., 1974.

Covner, B. S. Studies in the phonographic recorders of verbal material: III the completeness of accuracy of counselor interview reports. *Journal of General Psychology,* 1943, *30,* 181–203.

Cull, J., Colvin, C. *Contemporary field work practices in rehabilitation.* Springfield, Ill.: Charles C Thomas, 1972.

Demos, G. D. Suggested use of tape recordings in counseling supervision. *Personnel and Guidance Journal,* 1964, *42,* 704–5.

De la Torre, Jorge. Use and misuse of cliches in clinical supervision. *Archives of General Psychiatry,* 1974, *31,* 302–6.

Drucker, P. F. *The practice of management.* New York: Harper, 1976.

Duncan, M. G. An experiment in applying new methods in field work. *Social Casework, 1963, 44,* 179–84.

English, R. W., & Jelenevsky, S. Counselor behavior as judged under audio, visual, and audio-visual communication conditions. *Journal of Counseling Psychology,* 1971, *18,* 509–13.

Ferber, A., & Mendelsohn, M. Training for family therapy. *Family Process,* 1969, *8,* 25–32.

Finger, K. F. *Final report of the ADAMHA/NIAAA planning panel on alcoholism counselor credentialing.* Washington, D.C.: H.E.W. ADAMHA/NIAAA, 1977.

Fleischman, O. A method of teaching psychotherapy: One way vision room technique. *Bulletin of the Menninger Clinic, 1955, 19,* 160–72.

Friesen, D. D., & Dunning, G. B. Peer evaluation and practicum supervision. *Counselor Education and Supervision,* 1973, *13,* 229–35.

Froehlich, C. P. The completeness and accuracy of counseling interview reports. *Journal of General Psychology,* 1958, *58,* 84–96.

Gendlin, E. T. Experiencing: A variable in the process of therapeutic change. *American Journal of Psychotherapy,* 1961, *15,* 233–45.

Goin, M. K., & Kline, F. M. Supervision observed. *Journal of Nervous and Mental Disease,* 1974, *158,* 208–13.

Goldhammer, R. *Clinical supervision: Special methods for supervision of teachers.* New York: Holt, 1969.

Gordon, T. *Parent effectiveness training: P.E.T.* New York: Peter Wyden, 1970.

Gruenberg, P. B., Liston, E. H. Jr., & Wayne, G. J. Intensive supervision of psychotherapy with video-tape recording. *American Journal of Psychotherapy,* 1968, *23,* 95–105.

Gybers, N. C. Strategies for practicum supervision. *Counselor Education and Supervision,* 1964, *3,* 149–52.

Hallowitz, D. The supervisor as practicioner. *Social Casework,* 1962, *43,* 287–92.

Hare, R. T., & Frankena, S. T. Peer group supervision. *American Journal of Orthopsychiatry,* 1972, *42,* 527–29.

Hawthorne, L. Games supervisors play. *Social Work,* 1975, *20:* 179–83.

Hewer, V. An aid in supervision in practicum. *Journal of Counseling Psychology,* 1974, *21,* 66–70.

Hirsh, H., & Freed, H. Pattern sensitization in psychotherapy supervision by means of video-tape recording. In M. Berger (Ed.), *Video-tape techniques in psychiatric training and treatment.* New York: Bruner-Mazel, 1970.

Hora, T. Contribution to the phenomenology of the supervisory process. *American Journal of Psychotherapy,* 1957, *00,* 21, 769–773.

Itzin, F. The use of tape recording in field work. *Social Casework,* 1960, *41,* 197–202.

Judd, J., Kohn, R. E., & Shulman, G. L. Group supervision: A vehicle for professional development. *Social Work,* 1962 *7(1),* 96–102.

Kadushin, A. The effects of interview observation on the interviewer. *Journal of Counseling Psychology,* 1956, *3,* 130–35.

Kadushin, A. Interview observation as a teaching device. *Social Casework,* 1956, *37,* 334–41.

Kadushin, A. Games people play in supervision. *Social Work,* 1968, *13(3),* 23–32.

Kagan, N., Krathwohl, D. R., & Miller, R. Stimulated recall in therapy using video-tape: A case study. *Journal of Counseling Psychology,* 1963, *10,* 237–43.

Kennedy, M., & Keitner, L. What is supervision: The need for a redefinition. *Social Work,* 1970, *38,* 51–52.

Kohn, R. Differential use of observed interview in student training. *Social Work Education Reporter,* 1971, *19,* 45–46.

Lanning, W. L. A study of the relation between group and individual counseling supervision and three relationship measures. *Journal of Counseling Psychology,* 1971, *18,* 401–6.

Leader, A. L. Supervision and consultations through observed interviewing. *Social Casework,* 1968, *49,* 288–93.

Lister, J. L. Counselor experiencing: Its implications for supervision. Unpublished paper, 1965.

MacGuffie, R., Janzen, F. V., & McPhee, W. M. The expression and perception of feelings between students and supervisors in a practicum setting. *Counselor Education and Supervision,* 1970, *10,* 263–71.

Maier, N. R. F. *The appraisal interview.* New York: Wiley, 1958.

Marcus, P. M. Supervision and group process. *Human Organization,* 1961, *20,* 15–19.

Marohn, R. C. The similarity of therapy and supervision themes. *International Journal of Group Psychotherapy, 1969, 19,* 176–84.

Mattinson, J. The reflection process in casework supervision. Washington, D.C.: National Association of Social Workers, 1975.

McGoldrick, E. J. *The conquest of alcohol.* New York: Delacorte Press, 1966.

Medical College of Pennsylvania. Study of the needs for clinical supervision. Philadelphia: 1975.

Meerloo, J. A. M. Some processes in supervision of therapists. *American Journal of Orthopsychiatry,* 1952, *6,* 467–70.

Meyer, C. H. *Staff development in public welfare agencies.* New York: Columbia University Press, 1966.

Miller, C. D., & Oetting, E. R. Students react to supervision. *Counselor Education and Supervision, 1966, 6,* 73–4.

Montalvo, B. Aspects of live supervision. *Family Process,* 1973, *12,* 343–59.

Mosher, R. L., & Purpel, D. E. *Supervision: the reluctant profession.* Boston: Houghton, 1972.

Mozee, E. Counselor evaluate thyself. *The Personnel and Guidance Journal,* 1972, *51, 4,* 285–88.

Muslin, H. L., Burstein, A. G., Gedo, J. E., & Sadow, L. Research on the supervisory process. I. Supervisor's appraisal of the interview data. *Archives of General Psychiatry,* 1967, *16,* 427–31.

Nash, V. C. *The Clinical supervision of psychotherapy.* Unpublished Doctoral Dissertation. New Haven: Yale University, 1975.

Niland, T. M., Duling, J., Allen, J., & Panther, E. Student counselor's perception of video-taping. *Counselor Education and Supervision,* 1971, *11,* 97–101.

Paris, N. M. T groups and training counselors. *Human Relations Training Newsletter,* 1964, *8,* 13–14.

Payne, P. A., Winter, D. E., & Bell, G. E. Effects of supervision style on the learning of empathy in a separate analogue. *Counselor Education and Supervision,* 1972, *11,* 262–69.

Perlman, H. H. Teaching casework by the discussion method. *Social Service Review,* 1950, *24,* 334–46.

Pettes, D. E. *Supervision in social work.* London: Allan, 1967.

Pointer, A. Y., & Fishman, J. R. *New careers: Entry level training for the human service aide.* Washington, D.C.: New Careers Development Program, University Research Corporation, 1968.

Poling, E. G. Video-tape recordings in counseling practicum I, environmental considerations. *Counselor Education and Supervision,* 1968, *8,* 348–56.

Powell, D. J. *Manpower Needs in the Alcohol Field.* Bloomfield, Conn.: EAA-ETP, 1976.

Purvis, L. C. Self-awareness: A proposal for supervision. *Journal of Contemporary Psychotherapy,* 1972, *4,* 107–12.

Riessman, F., & Goldfarb, J. Role playing and the poor. *Group Psychotherapy,* 1964, *17,* 36–48.

Riessman, F., & Goldfarb, J. Strategies and suggestions for training nonprofessionals. *Community Mental Health Journal,* 1972, *3,* 103–10.

Rioch, M. J. Changing concepts in the training of therapists. *Journal of Consulting Psychology,* 1966, *30,* 290–92.

Rosenbaum, M. Problems in supervision of psychiatric residents in psychotherapy. *Archives of Neurological Psychiatry,* 1953, *69,* 43–8.

Ryan, C. Video-aids in practicum supervision. *Counselor Education and Supervision,* 1969, *8,* 125–29.

Ryan, F. Joint interviewing by field instructors and students. *Social Casework,* 1964, *45,* 471–74.

Searles, H. F. The informational value of the supervisor's emotional experiences. *Psychiatry,* 1955, *18,* 135–46.

Seegars, J. E. & McDonald, R. L. The role of interaction groups in counselor education. *Journal of Counseling Psychology,* 1963, *10,* 156–62.

Sharaf, M. R., & Levinson, D. J. The quest for omnipotence in professional training. *Psychiatry,* 1964, *27,* 135–49.

Sobey, F. *The non-professional revolution in mental health.* New York: Columbia University Press, 1970.

Stier, S., & Goldenberg, I. Training issues in family therapy. *Journal of Marriage and Family Counseling,* 1976, *2,* 269–276.

Strecker, E. A., & Chambers, F. T. *Alcohol—one man's meat.* New York: MacMillan, 1939.

Suess, J. F. Self-confrontation of video-taped psychotherapy as a teaching device for psychiatric students. *Journal of Medical Education,* 1970, *45,* 271–82.

Towle, C. *The learner in education for the professions: as seen in education for social workers.* Chicago: University of Chicago Press, 1954.

Truax, C. B., Carkhuff, R. R., & Douds, J. Toward an integration of the didactic and experiential approaches to training in counseling and psychotherapy. *Journal of Counseling Psychology,* 1964, *11,* 240–47.

Van Atta, R. E. Co-therapy as a supervisory process. *Psychotherapy: Theory, Research, and Practice,* 1969, *6,* 137–9.

Van Atta, R. E. Excitory and inhibitory effect of various modes of observation in counseling. *Journal of Counseling Psychology,* 1969, *16,* 433–39.

Vermont Alcohol Counselor's Association, Inc. *Ethical standards of alcohol counselors.* Unpublished paper, 1978.

Walz, G. R., & Johnston, J. A. Counselors look at themselves on video-tape. *Journal of Counseling Psychology,* 1963, *10,* 232–36.

Ward, C. H. Electronic preceptoring in teaching beginning psychotherapy. *Journal of Medical Education,* 1962, *37,* 1128–29.

Watson, K. W. Differential supervision. *Social Work,* 1973, *18,* (6), 80–88.

Wax, J. Time-limited supervision. *Social Work,* 8 (3): 37–43, 1963.

Wilkie, C. H. A study of distortions in recording interviews. *Social Work,* 1963, *8,* 31–36.

Williamson, M. *Supervision: new patterns and processes.* New York: Association Press, 1961.

Worby, C. First year psychiatric residents and the professional identity crisis. *Mental Hygiene,* 1970, *54,* 374–377.

Yalom, I. D. *The theory and practice of group psychotherapy.* New York: Basic Books, 1970.

Zetzel, E. The dynamic basis of supervision. *Social Casework,* 1953, *34,* 143–49.

Zimmy, G. H., Brown, J. E., Ellis, J. J., & Sorenson, J. C. The use of television in the clinical internship programs. *Professional Psychology,* 1972, *3,* 271–76.

REFERENCES

Aiken, J., Smits, S., and Lollar, D. J. Leadership behavior and job satisfaction in state rehabilitation agencies. *Personnal Psychology,* 1972, 25, 65–73.

Briefland, D., Briggs, T. L., and Leuenberger, P. *The team model of social work practice.* Syracuse, N.Y.: Syracuse University School of Social Work, 1973.

Bruner, J. S. *The process of education.* New York: Random House, 1963.

Caplan, S. *The theory and practice of mental health consultation.* New York: Basic Books, 1970.

Ekstein, R., and Wallerstein, R. S. *The teaching and learning of psychotherapy.* 2nd Ed. New York: International Universities Press, 1972.

Epstein, I. Professionalization, professionalism, and social worker radicalism. *J. of Health and Social Behavior,* 11, 67–77, 1970.

Edelwich, J. *Counselor Burnout.* Unpublished paper, 1978.

Finger, K. H. *Final report of the ADAMHA/NIAAA planning panel on alcoholism counselors.* Washington, D.C.: National Institute on Alcohol Abuse and Alcoholism, DHEW, unpublished report, 1977.

Fleisher, D. S. Priorities and data bases: their relationship to continuing education. In: *Fostering the growing need to learn.* HSM 110-71-147, July, 1973.

Fleming, J., and Benedek, T. *Psychoanalytic supervision.* New York: Grune, 1966.

Henry, W. E., Sims, J. H., and Spray, L. S. *The fifth profession.* San Francisco: Jossey-Bass, 1971.

Kadushin, A. *Supervision in social work.* New York: Columbia University Press, 1973.

Kaslow, F. W. Group Supervision. In: F. W. Kaslow and associates, *Issues in Human services.* San Francisco: Jossey-Bass, 1972, pp. 115–141.

Kermish, I., and Kushin, F. Why high turnover? Social work staff losses in a county welfare agency. *Public Welfare,* 1969, 27, 134–37.

Maslow, A. H. *Motivation and personality,* 2nd Ed. New York: Harper and Row, 1970.

Medical College of Pennsylvania study on clinical supervision. Philadelphia, Pa.: unpublished report, 1976.

Miller, G. E. Continuing education for what? *J. of Med. Ed.,* 1967, 42, 320–23.

Miller, S. *Components of job satisfaction for beginning social workers.* Mimeographed. Kalamazoo, Michigan: School of Social Work, Western Michigan University, 1970.

Maier, N. R. F. Three types of appraisal interview, In: N. R. F. Maier, *The appraisal interview.* New York: Wiley, 1958.

Mueller, W. J. and Kell, B. L. *Coping with conflict: Supervising counselors and psychotherapists.* New York: Appleton-Century-Crofts, 1972.

NIAAA proposed standards for alcoholism counselor certification. Washington, D.C.: National Institute on Alcohol Abuse and Alcoholism, DHEW, unpublished report, 1974.

Olmstead, J. and Christensen, H. E. Effects of agency work contexts: An intensive field study. *Research Report #2* Washington D.C.: DHEW Social and Rehabilitation Service, 1973.

Rapoport, L. The use of supervision as a tool in professional development. *British J. of Psychiatric Social Work,* 1954, 2, 66–74.

Rogers, C. R. Training individuals to engage in the therapeutic process. In: C. R. Strether, Ed. *Psychology and mental health.* Washington, D.C. American Psychological Association, 1957.

Rogers, C. R. *Client-centered therapy: Its current practice, implications and theory.* Boston: Houghton-Mifflin Co., 1951.

Rowley, C. and Faux, E. The team approach to supervision. *Mental Hygiene,* 1966, 50, 60–65.

Sales, E., and Navarre, E. *Individual and group supervision in field instruction: A research report.* Ann Arbor, Michigan, School of Social Work, University of Michigan, 1970.

Schuster, D. B. Sandt, J. J., and Thaler, O. F. *Clinical supervision of psychiatric residents.* New York: Bruner/Mazel, 1970.

Strecker, E. A., and Chambers, F. T. *Alcohol: One Man's Meat.* New York: McMillan, 1938.

Szasz, T. S. *The myth of mental illness: Foundations of a theory of personal conflict.* New York: Hoeber-Harper, 1966.

Tillich, P. *On the boundary.* New York: Charles Scribner's Sons, 1966.

Truax, C. B. and Carkhuff, R. R. *Toward effective counseling and psychotherapy training and practice.* Chicago: Aldine, 1967.

Tucker, S. M. *Sequential model for clinical supervision.* New York: New York University. Unpublished doctoral dissertation, 1976.

Valle, S. *Alcoholism counseling: Issues for an emerging profession.* Springfield, Ill.: Charles C. Thomas, 1979.

Watson, K. W. Differential supervision. *Social Work,* 1973, 18, 80–8.

INDEX